NEW YORK
HEART OF THE CITY

J. P. MacBean

MALLARD PRESS

An Imprint of BDD Promotional Book Company
666 Fifth Avenue
New York, N.Y. 10103

MALLARD PRESS
An imprint of
BDD Promotional Book Company, Inc.
666 Fifth Avenue
New York, N.Y. 10103

Mallard Press and its accompanying design and logo are trademarks of
BDD Promotional Book Company, Inc.

First published in the United States of America in 1990 by Mallard Press.

Printed and bound in Spain

ISBN 0-792-45095-7

Author: J.P. MacBean
Producer: Solomon M. Skolnick
Designer: Barbara Cohen Aronica
Editor: Madelyn Larsen
Production Coordinator: Ann-Louise Lipman
Picture Researcher: Edward Douglas
Production Assistant: Valerie Zars
Assistant Picture Researcher: Robert V. Hale

Title page: **The Twin Towers of the World Trade Center.**

The Statue of Liberty, the gift of the people of France to the people of the United States, has become a universal symbol of freedom.

◄◄ Clockwise from top left:

A new golden torch was added when the Statue of Liberty was completely renovated for her 100th birthday in 1986. The old torch is now on display in the statue's base.

The statue's crown can hold up to 40 people. Visitors, who must climb about 100 feet up a winding staircase to reach the head, are rewarded with breathtaking views of New York Harbor and the Manhattan skyline.

The seven spikes in the crown represent the seven seas and seven continents. During the 1986 restoration of the statue, the angle of one spike had to be changed because it had worn a hole in the copper skin of the Lady's upraised arm.

◄ Ellis Island, which served as an immigrant station from 1892 until 1954, processed some 12,000,000 U.S. citizens. As a result, it is estimated that 40% of all Americans have Ellis Island roots.

▼ For the millions of immigrants who sailed into New York Harbor after 1886, the Statue of Liberty welcomed them with her promise of freedom and hope in the new land.

PLANTING THE BIG APPLE

When visitors reach the top of New York City's two highest man-made mountains—the World Trade Center and the Empire State Building—the word that most frequently comes to mind is . . . incredible! First-timers will often say it out loud, but even repeat visitors or long-time residents will *think* it. How can they help it? Spread out before them is one of the world's most amazing sights. Towers rise in clusters, like stalagmites left by a giant's day of building sand castles at the beach. Water is everywhere, a confluence of rivers, inlets, tidal basins, bays, and ocean. Bridges—large and small, old and new, sixty-five in all— strain to tie and hold together five vastly different boroughs. The density and diversity of hundreds of different neighborhoods in these five boroughs—Manhattan, Brooklyn, Queens, Staten Island, and The Bronx—set the mind spinning. And all around, wherever you look—in the air, on the waters and on the streets far below—planes are arriving every minute, ships and boats and ferries are plying the rivers and bays, the traffic is forever streaming, and the people are constantly scurrying.

How did this miracle city happen? Who did it all? And when? The incredibility of New York only deepens when you realize that almost everything you can see from your perch at the Empire State Building or Tower 1 of the World Trade Center is less than one hundred years old. The Woolworth Building, that graceful Gothic spire in lower Manhattan, rose in 1913; and its near neighbor, the New York Stock Exchange, the very symbol of the financial district, is just slightly older (1903). Landmarks like the Chrysler Building, Rockefeller Center, and the Empire State Building itself (and who can think of New York without them?) are all products of the 1930s; and several other indispensable parts of the city's political, cultural and business life did not arrive until later decades: the United Nations (1947–53), Lincoln Center for the Performing Arts (1962–68), and the World Trade Center (1962–77). It always amuses visitors from abroad to hear New Yorkers boast about the city's "old, historic sights" such as St. Patrick's Cathedral (1879), the Metropolitan Museum of Art (begun in 1880 and still building), the Brooklyn Bridge (1883), the Statue of Liberty (1886), and Carnegie Hall (1891). Even Broadway, which translates into "the theater" around the world, cannot point to one existing nineteenth-century house. The oldest survivor, The Lyceum (1903), an ornate, neo-Baroque beauty on West 45th Street, is indeed a treasure, but try impressing anyone from Athens with its age.

▶ Top to bottom:

A magic island of architectural wonders greets commuters and visitors who travel into the Battery at lower Manhattan on the Staten Island Ferry.

The Staten Island Ferry, which is part of New York City's public transportation system, regularly plies between the tip of lower Manhattan and the St. George Ferry Terminal. The trip takes about 20 minutes, and is one of the finest sightseeing cruises in the world.

Sprays from a New York fireboat are a traditional welcome to visiting cruise ships and naval vessels, especially if a holiday celebration is in progress.

▶▶ Skyline of lower Manhattan.

(preceding pages) The towers of lower Manhattan, the city's oldest and most historic area and now its financial center.

◄ Top to bottom:

The weathered copper covering of this ferry slip at the Battery gives the structure its greenish hue.

Battery Park in spring, a haven for office workers at lunchtime.

A new city rises on the Hudson River landfill that was taken from the excavations of the World Trade Center, with the beautiful buildings of the World Financial Center as its most outstanding feature.

► Cesar Pelli, the architect of the World Financial Center, has created forms that are both practical and pleasing to the eye.

You can, of course, find truly impressive old monuments, houses and buildings throughout the city: the 1680 "Conference House" in Staten Island, where Benjamin Franklin, John Adams and others met with the British in an unsuccessful attempt to resolve the War of Independence; the 1694 Friends' Meeting House in the Flushing neighborhood of Queens, now a Quaker landmark of religious freedom; and the 1765 Morris-Jumel Mansion in Washington Heights, which was used at various times during the Revolution as a headquarters for both George Washington and the British forces. You can even find a house in Greenwich Village that barely squeaks by as eighteenth century. But you are really brought up short when you learn that the only existing pre-Revolutionary public building in New York is St. Paul's Chapel in lower Manhattan (1764), where George Washington worshipped following his first inauguration as president on April 30, 1789. Even nearby Fraunces Tavern, originally an eighteenth-century building where Washington bade farewell to his troops, stands today as a 1907 reconstruction.

The sad story here is that only in the past few decades—with the arrival of organizations like the Landmarks Commission, the Friends of Cast-Iron Architecture and the Municipal Art Society—have New Yorkers been prompted to preserve their heritage before it vanishes forever. Previously, the city's unofficial motto was "down with the old and up with the new." Reverence for the historic was Old World; progress was the driving force of the New World.

Appropriately, the ethnic diversity that characterizes and enriches the city today was present at its birth and guided its growth. First of all, before the sixteenth century, Native Americans, among them the Algonquin, the Iroquois, and the Manhattoe, lived off the land and fished its rich waters. The first European to enter what is now New York Bay, in April 1524, was Giovanni da Verrazano, an Italian explorer serving the French King Francis I. Next year, in January 1525, Estéban Gómez, a Portuguese navigator in the service of the Spanish King Charles, also investigated the bay area. Neither Verrazano nor Gómez made any effort to colonize the area—in fact, there is no record that they ever set foot on its land—but the former is remembered today by the magnificent Verrazano-Narrows Bridge (1964) that spans the opening of the bay between the boroughs of Brooklyn and Staten Island.

The third and most important explorer added two more nationalities to the area's ethnic history. Henry Hudson, an English navigator employed by the Dutch East India Company, guided the *Half Moon* into the lower Bay on September 2, 1609.

(preceding pages) Older buildings of lower Manhattan frame the towers of the new World Financial Center, which stretches along the Hudson River waterfront next to the World Trade Center.

► The Woolworth Building (top), a Neo-Gothic masterpiece opposite City Hall in lower Manhattan, was the tallest building in the world when it rose in 1913. New York City skyscrapers (bottom) are a study in contrast: to the right is the Gothic tower of the Woolworth Building, to the left are the Twin Towers of the World Trade Center, built in the 1960s.

►► The Woolworth Building (foreground) complements the larger, more elaborate Municipal Building (background), which holds numerous offices of the City government.

▲ This Greek Revival edifice (1834–42) once served as a custom house and subtreasury building. Now Federal Hall National Memorial, it marks the site of George Washington's first inaugural.

◄ This heroic statue of George Washington by J.Q.A. Ward marks the spot where the first president of the United States took his oath of office on April 30, 1789.

This time the exploration "took." Hudson anchored his ship and, in the course of the next few weeks, explored what is now Manhattan Island and introduced himself to the inhabitants. Later on, he sailed north, exploring the banks of the great river that now bears his name.

THE DUTCH COLONIAL ERA

Hudson's Dutch employers were delighted with his discoveries—especially his reports of the land's wealth in fur-bearing animals. Colonization proceeded at a fairly rapid rate: the Dutch explorer and trader Adriaen Block spent the winter of 1613–14 on Manhattan, and over the next few years the first Dutch colonists built huts and a simple fortification called Fort Amsterdam. In 1624, Dutch and Walloon settlers (the latter were French-speaking Protestants fleeing persecution in the Spanish Netherlands, an area occupied today by southern Belgium) solidified the foothold in Manhattan and other spots throughout the area, including Brueckelen, or Brooklyn, as it is now known; and in 1625 the first permanent settlement was named Nieuw Amsterdam.

The purchase of Manhattan from the Manhattoe Indians supposedly took place in 1626, when Peter Minuit, governor of the new settlement, sealed the deal for "cloth and fripperies

worth about twenty-four dollars." Certain scholars doubt the transaction. For one thing, the Indians had no concept of land ownership as we know it; in all probability, the Native Americans were simply allowing our forebears to share their paradise and its natural resources. In any case, the "sale" makes a good story, one that comedians could not do without and one that has been immortalized in the 1939 Rodgers and Hart song, "Give It Back to the Indians." Bowling Green, at the foot of Broadway in lower Manhattan, is the putative location for the historic event. It is the city's oldest public park and has recently been beautifully restored.

Peter ("Pegleg Pete") Stuyvesant, the Dutch era's most prominent and most colorful figure, became Director General of Nieuw Amsterdam in 1647. Under his astute leadership, the settlement was recognized as a town, a wooden wall was built to protect the colony's northern boundary (Wall Street marks the spot today), and the first permanent Jewish settlement in the colonies was established. By this time there were other Dutch villages throughout the area, including settlements on what we now know as Queens and Staten Island. In 1639, a Danish immigrant named Jonas Bronck bought 500 acres of land from the Dutch West India Company, and that's why New York City's northernmost borough—and the only one on the mainland— is called The Bronx.

Throughout the four decades of Dutch rule, the English and the Dutch were highly competitive trading rivals, and England was by no means oblivious to the Dutch colony's importance in political and social terms. Furthermore, New Amsterdam was a far from stable colony: the inhabitants and their governors

▲ The handsome exterior of the New York Stock Exchange, 8 Broad Street, just below Wall Street, was designed by George B. Post and features a classic pediment by J.Q.A. Ward.

▶ A typical day's trading on the floor of the Exchange.

were constantly at loggerheads. Therefore, some sort of upheaval was inevitable.

The end of Dutch rule came in 1664, when a British war fleet sailed into port and demanded the town's surrender in the name of the Duke of York. (Apparently, King Charles II, the duke's brother, had given him a grant that included all of what we now know as New York State and large parts of New England, so the duke was simply staking out his claim.) Pegleg Pete tried to rally his querulous fellow citizens, but the good burghers—with perhaps more practicality than patriotism—decided to capitulate without a struggle. Overnight New Amsterdam turned into New York.

Although the Dutch held sway for only forty years, they certainly left their mark on the cultural, political, and social fabrics of the city. The north Manhattan neighborhood of Harlem is known around the world, and the name Bloomingdale (from *bloemendael*, "vale of flowers") lives on in one of New York's most chic department stores. The Bowery (from Peter Stuyvesant's *bouwerij*, or "farm") is now a catch phrase for skid row; New Yorkers still eat crullers (from *krullen*, those twists of deep-fat-fried sweet dough), and New York town houses still have stoops (from the Dutch *stoep*). Minetta Lane, named for Minetta Brook (originally *Mintje Kill*, or "small stream") which still flows somewhere beneath it, is one of Greenwich Village's most charming byways; and Stuyvesant Square is a handsome oasis on the Lower East Side. Beaver Street, in the Wall Street area, memorializes the animal that provided the basis of the city's early economy (it appeared on the provincial seal of Nieuw Nederland, 1623–64), and a beaver is also the motif of the tile

mosaics in the East Village's Astor Place subway station. (John Jacob Astor, at one time the city's richest man, built his fortune on the beaver trade.)

Knickerbocker Holiday, the delightful 1938 musical by Maxwell Anderson and Kurt Weill, is loosely based on the goings-on in mid-seventeenth-century New Amsterdam; Walter Huston, who sang the classic "September Song," was unforgettable as Pegleg Pete Stuyvesant. The irrepressible old governor is buried in the graveyard of the 1799 St. Mark's-in-The-Bowerie (1799), which stands on the site of the former Stuyvesant estate. If you go to pay your respects, also take a look at the handsome 1804 Stuyvesant-Fish Residence at nearby 21 Stuyvesant Street; then stroll up and down Second Avenue in the East Village, see the old Yiddish theater Rialto. . .which is another story in another era of Little Old New York.

BRITISH RULE BEGINS

The British, ever the efficient colonizers, wasted no time in anglicizing their new colony. English government, the English language, and the Church of England were immediately established as the standards for New York's political, social, and religious life.

During the next hundred years, the colony grew and prospered, although it was not until after the Revolution that New York

►► Trinity Church's soaring Gothic interior is often the scene of free lunchtime concerts. A small museum, off to the left, explains the church's history.

▼ The steeple of St. Paul's Chapel *(top)* rises in front of the Twin Towers of the World Trade Center. Designed by Thomas McBean, St. Paul's is the only pre-Revolutionary public building left in New York. Trinity Church *(bottom)* as seen through the canyon of Wall Street. The original building was burned during the American Revolution; this Neo-Gothic structure dates from 1846.

City began to grow rapidly into the megapolis it is today. (No exact figures are available, but pre-Revolutionary New York probably contained fewer than 25,000 people, most of them living in Manhattan.)

Important events during this time of growth include the movement of the seat of government in 1701 from the old Dutch City Hall (Stadt Huys) on Pearl Street to a new city hall at the juncture of Broad and Wall streets. A block away, Trinity Church was founded in 1696, built in 1698, and renovated in 1737 (before being completely burned during the Revolution). Thanks to Queen Anne's original grant in 1705, Trinity became the colony's largest landowner, its property stretching from Fulton to Christopher streets, and from Broadway to the Hudson River.

New York's first synagogue, serving the colonies' first Jewish settlement, was established in 1729 on Beaver Street; and the first New York college, King's College (now Columbia University), was founded in 1754. Historians are still debating the date and place of New York's first theater, some hold that it arrived in 1732 on Maiden Lane (named for the path that young girls used to take to the brook where they did the family laundry). Research done by Helen Hayes for her book with Anita Loos, *Twice Over Lightly,* found that the first (and nameless) theater opened March 11, 1779, with an offering called *Ye Old Beggerman and His Termagant Landlady*.

THE ROAD TO REVOLUTION

The press has always played a large role in the life of the city—ever since William Bradford founded New York's first newspaper, the *New-York Gazette* in 1725. Long before the First Amendment to the United States Constitution guaranteed freedom of speech, one of the most important events in the nation's history took place in 1735 at City Hall (the spot now marked by Federal Hall National Memorial, which is also the site of George Washington's inauguration as first president). Editor-journalist John Peter Zenger, who had started the *New-York Weekly Journal* in 1733–34, dared to oppose the royal governor and his colonial policy. In 1735, some of Zenger's published writings were burned in public and he was imprisoned and charged with slander. His acquittal, in a famous "freedom of the press" trial, is credited with laying the foundations of one of the most important rights we enjoy as U.S. citizens.

In spite of the colony's general prosperity and great promise, England, as numerous events indicated, was having serious problems maintaining order and stability in New York. The Dutch, in a brief 1673 episode, recaptured New York without a struggle and renamed it New Orange (after the House of Orange), but this diversion ended the very next year when the colony was returned to the English under the Treaty of Westminster. Far more troublesome were the constant and growing competition with the French in matters both political and practical, the always-present threat of hostile Indian tribes, and, of course, the colonies' growing resentment at Britain's dominance and its oppressive policies. No sooner did the Treaty of Paris end the French and Indian Wars in 1763, thereby establishing English control of North America, than a 1765 meeting of the Stamp Act Congress in New York denounced the practice of "taxation without representation." The Stamp Act was repealed in 1766, as were the Townshend Acts of 1767, which had *increased* taxation and curtailed self-government—but the seeds of revolution had been planted and were being nurtured daily.

▲ Free outdoor concerts are a regular feature in the vast outdoor plaza in front of the Winter Garden in the World Financial Center.

◄ Sixteen living palm trees are planted in the polished marble lobby of the Winter Garden.

◄◄ Weather-worn tombstones in the graveyard of St. Paul's Chapel represent the old New York; the massive towers of the World Trade Center are the city of the present and future.

▼ "Sphere for Plaza Fountain" by Fritz Koenig is the centerpiece of the World Trade Center's Austin J. Tobin Plaza.

When the Declaration of Independence was pronounced in Philadelphia by the Continental Congress on July 4, 1776, a copy, rushed to New York by courier, was read to the citizens gathered on the City Common (now City Hall Park) in the presence of George Washington. By the end of the year, the city would be overrun, burned, and taken captive, which it remained until the British evacuation at the end of the War of Independence in 1783.

THE REVOLUTION MARCHES ACROSS NEW YORK

The war struck New York with a sword that was both terrible and swift. In fairly rapid succession, following the July 4th Declaration of Independence, the British won the Battle of Long Island, and on August 27 they drove General George Washington's troops across Brooklyn and the East River into Manhattan, whence the Continentals were forced to retreat to northern Manhattan. Here General Washington tasted a sweet but brief victory in the Battle of Harlem Heights, before the British overran Fort Washington on November 17, 1776. Thus ended the war as far as New York City's active military involvement was concerned.

Even though its single year as a battlefield of the war was fleeting, the Revolution's New York City chapter nevertheless contains some stirring episodes.

Nathan Hale, a twenty-one-year-old Yale graduate and fledgling schoolteacher, became, through a single act of heroism, one of the Revolution's most exemplary heroes. As a captain in Washington's army, he volunteered to obtain information from behind British lines on Long Island. In one of history's most obvious examples of typecasting, he went on the mission disguised as . . . a schoolmaster. The plot failed; Hale was discovered and hanged without trial as a self-confessed spy on September 22, 1776. Historians disagree about the site of the young patriot's execution. Some point to First Avenue and 45th or 46th Street, others to 44th Street and Vanderbilt Avenue, site of today's Yale Club. Other authorities say the hanging took place near the old Dove Tavern at 65th Street and Third Avenue (today, the tavern site is occupied by the Sign of the Dove restaurant). There are scholars who also doubt that Nathan Hale ever actually uttered his famous gallows line ("I regret that I have but one life to lose for my country!"). A well-known statue of Nathan Hale, the work of Frederick MacMonnies, stands to the left of City Hall.

Among New York's war heroes, female honors go to Mary Lindley Murray, wife of the Quaker Robert Murray, who owned almost all of the area now called Murray Hill. When the Battle of Long Island was lost and General Washington's troops were forced to flee across the East River and up the east side of Manhattan Island, it was Mary Lindley Murray who provided the delaying action necessary for the Continentals to escape the pursuing British troops. She invited British General William Howe to tarry over tea at her country home, located at what is now 37th Street and Park Avenue, thereby saving the day. Again, scholars doubt the details of this delightful story—holding that General Howe had decided to stop for refreshments anyway—but how often legend is more interesting than fact!

After the war, the Murray estate was divided into lots, and by the late nineteenth century it had become the neighborhood where many of Society's "The Four Hundred" lived. Landmarks of the area worth noting are the J. P. Morgan home and library (a museum at 33 East 36th Street) and the Sniffen Court Historic District (a delightful mews of mid-nineteenth-century

(preceding pages) Patterns in the sky, patterns in the skyscrapers. From these heights at the World Trade Center, King Kong plunged to the plaza in the 1977 remake of the original film classic.

◄ ◄ To some, Fritz Koenig's spherical sculpture at the World Trade Center's Plaza resembles an abstract Atlas holding up the world.

(following pages) The Financial District, a mélange of distinctive buildings that power the nation and some say the world.

▼ The central hall of the Surrogate's Court/Hall of Records building *(top)* is an example of Beaux Arts design. Manhattan's Municipal Building *(bottom)*, seen here through the park in front of City Hall, is the City government's main office building.

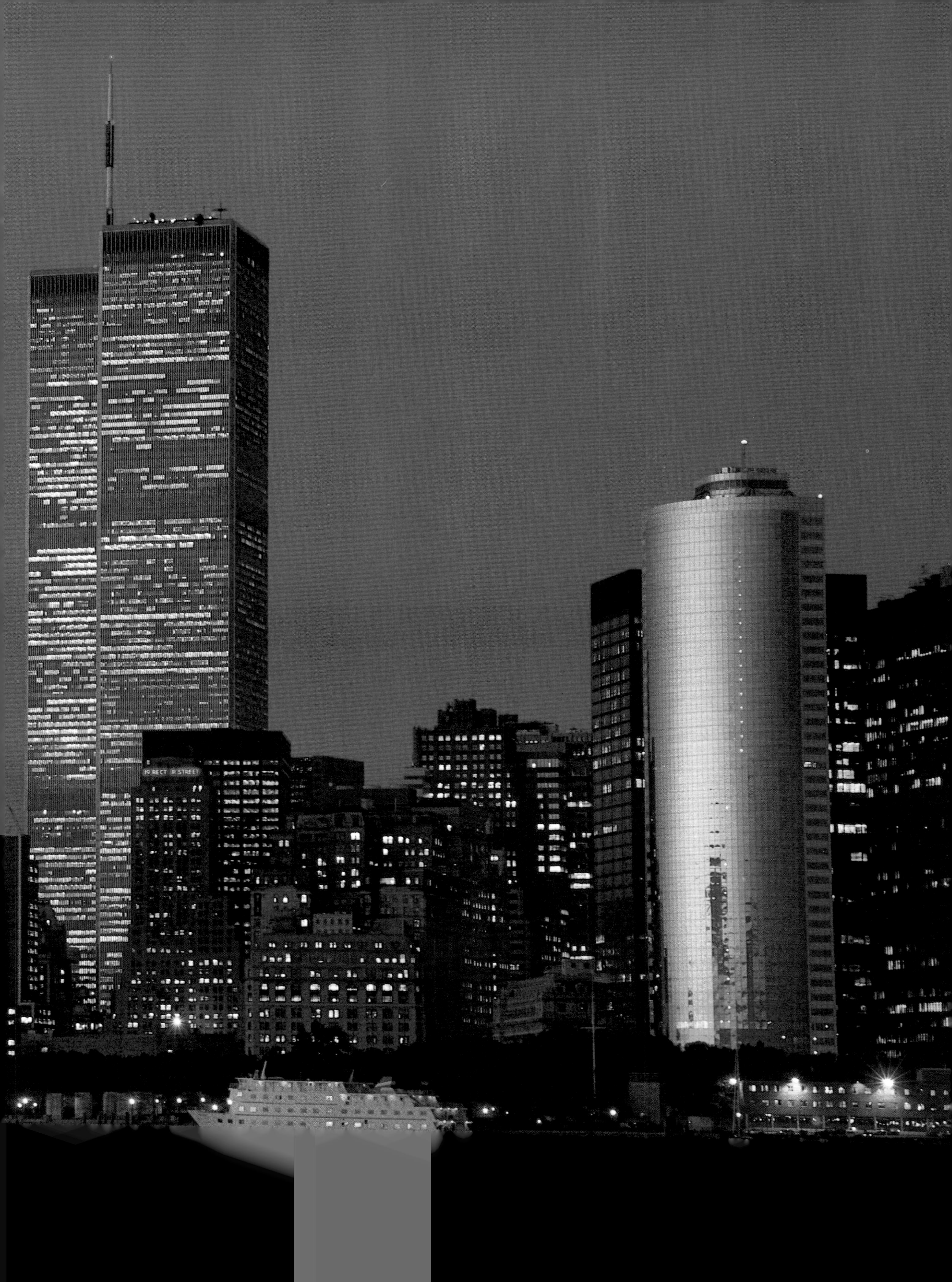
19 RECT R STREET

▲ A "side-wheeler" of the Seaport Line takes visitors to the South Street Seaport on excursions around New York Harbor.

◄ The great Brooklyn Bridge (1883), the first bridge to connect Manhattan and Brooklyn, is one of the city's most beloved attractions.

▼ The South Street Seaport is a haven for historic ships, including the Ambrose Lightship that used to guard the entrance to New York Harbor.

▲ Visitors to Pier 17 at the South Street Seaport can dine, drink, listen to street performers, laugh at comedians or just sit, relax, and take in the river views and salt air.

▼ By night, the ships and new pier buildings of the South Street Seaport are illuminated for the benefit of visitors to the area's numerous restaurants and clubs.

Hot mulled cider, to warm the hand and the heart, is just one of the treats available at the myriad food stalls, cafés, clubs, restaurants, and bars of the South Street Seaport.

carriage houses now converted to private homes). Another is the "Little Church Around the Corner" (1849–61); a "country parish," at 1 East 29th Street, it has been known as the actors' church ever since it agreed to conduct burial services for thespian George Holland in 1870, after fashionable Madison Avenue churches had refused to do so.

One has to look sharply among the commercial towers and residential buildings of modern New York for other traces of Revolutionary War days. Often only an approximate address is left, with not even a plaque to mark the historic spot. Bowling Green, in lower Manhattan, was the site of a rather impressive statue of George III that was torn down and melted to make bullets by the Liberty Boys. Remnants of the statue can be seen at the New-York Historical Society, Central Park West at 76th Street. Union Square, at Fifth Avenue and 14th Street, contains a bronze equestrian statue of George Washington by Henry Kirke Brown; it was dedicated on July 4, 1856, to mark the spot where Washington was received by New Yorkers following the evacuation of the city by the British on November 25, 1783.

The lovely King-Charlton-Vandam Historic District in Manhattan's Greenwich Village area is indeed historic ground. Here stood "Richmond Hill" (a plaque on the 1902 Butterick Building on the northwest corner of Spring Street and Avenue of the Americas marks the spot); this mansion, built in 1760 by Abraham Mortier, served as headquarters to General George Washington and later

as home to vice-presidents John Adams and Aaron Burr. The early nineteenth-century houses along King, Charlton, and Vandam streets are among the finest in New York City.

The Morris-Jumel Mansion of 1765 still stands at West 160th Street and Edgecombe Avenue in Washington Heights. During the War, the mansion served as headquarters for both General George Washington and the British forces. The house, a handsome Georgian-Federal summer residence, was built by Colonel Roger Morris and was later owned by Stephen Jumel, whose widow married Aaron Burr. (Burr, a controversial figure in American history, was vice-president under Thomas Jefferson; he shot and killed Alexander Hamilton, the former Secretary of the Treasury and a political opponent, in a duel on July 11, 1804. Dr. David Hosack, the physician who attended Hamilton, was the owner of the 20-acre Elgin Botanic Gardens, which were located where Rockefeller Center now stands.)

Northwest of Harlem, in Manhattan's Washington Heights section, stands Fort Tryon Park, scene of the Continental Army's last stand before being driven from New York. The magnificent site of the ramparts, overlooking the majestic Hudson River and the stunning New Jersey Palisades, is marked by a plaque that reads: "The northern outwork of Fort Washington. Its gallant defense against the Hessian Troops by the Maryland and Virginia Regiment, 16 November 1776, was shared by Margaret Corbin, the first American woman to take a soldier's part in the War for

Liberty.'' The Hessians mentioned in the inscription were soldiers in the service of German landgraves, who hired them out to the British to help fight the Continentals.

Fort Tryon Park, a gift of the Rockefeller family to New York City, is also the site of The Cloisters, a branch of The Metropolitan Museum of Art. Among its medieval treasures are French and Spanish monastic cloisters (imported and reassembled), Gothic and Romanesque chapels, and the incomparable Unicorn tapestries.

The 1748 Van Cortlandt House, located in Van Cortlandt Park in The Bronx, was another of Washington's headquarters during the Revolution; his troops camped here following the retreat from Long Island. Restored by the Colonial Dames, the fieldstone country house—with its intriguing kitchen, Dutch room and fine collection of Delft—is open to the public. In Fort Greene Park, Brooklyn, the Prison Ship Martyrs' Monument, designed by Stanford White, is a 148-foot granite shaft commemorating 11,000 patriots who suffered horrible deaths from starvation, disease, and abuse while held captive aboard British ships in the harbor.

► A *trompe l'oeil* wall mural of the Brooklyn Bridge mocks the real McCoy looming above it. You'll find the tricky picture at the northern end of the South Street Seaport.

◄ ▼ Fish comes in fresh each day—in the wee hours of the morning at the Fulton Fish Market, now part of the overall 12-block South Street Seaport complex. Restaurateurs and fishmongers arrive early to select the very best and freshest fish for their customers.

Following the Revolution, most British place and street names—at least all those with a royalist ring—were either Americanized or changed to honor those who had aided the cause of independence (e.g., Lafayette Street for the Marquis de Lafayette, the French hero; Sullivan Street for Brigadier General John Sullivan, one of the Colonials' ablest commanders; Pitt Street and Chatham Square for William Pitt, Earl of Chatham, who supported American opposition to the Stamp Act).

But don't be fooled by what may look like a British name. York Avenue on Manhattan's East Side was not named for the Duke of York but for Sergeant Alvin C. York, a most famous World War I hero. And King Street in the South Village has no royal connotation; it was named for Rufus King, a member of the Continental Congress and New York's first U.S. Senator.

It must be understood that not all of the colonists supported the Revolutionary War or independence. Some remained Loyalists, faithful to Tory principles; they included prosperous merchants and Southern plantation owners who wanted to maintain a steady market for their cotton crops in the English mills. Yet almost all clear thinkers at the time realized that a split

◄ Hart Crane and other American poets rhapsodized about the strength and grace of the Brooklyn Bridge, and generations of painters have fallen in love with the web-like beauty of its shimmering cables and wires.

► Gothic towers—or stone pylons—moor the Brooklyn and Manhattan ends of the Brooklyn Bridge.

▼ Designed by John A. Roebling, the Brooklyn Bridge is an example of brilliant design married to inspired engineering.

▲ Sailing under the Brooklyn Bridge in a vessel out of South Street Seaport is an exciting way to view the structure. A Circle Line cruise around Manhattan Island offers the same vantage points.

▶ ▶ Manhattan Bridge, just to the north of Brooklyn Bridge, frames the Empire State Building in the distance.

(preceding pages) About New York's great bridge, art historian Kenneth Clark said that "all modern New York, heroic New York, started with the Brooklyn Bridge."

from British rule was inevitable. The gulfs between the Old World and the New—political, social, philosophic, esthetic, and, especially, economic—were getting wider all the time. Besides, the New World was simply too big, and its people were individuals, not subjects. Under such circumstances, there was nothing Britain could do to maintain her control.

THE NATION'S FIRST CAPITAL

Once The Treaty of Paris formally ended the War of Independence, the thirteen colonies set about drafting a Constitution that would enumerate the rights they had fought for and establish a government to guarantee those rights.

During this critical period when the United States of America took shape, Philadelphia—as the site of the Federal Constitutional Convention of 1787—was in the spotlight. Nevertheless, New York City played a significant role in the forging of a nation, as the following significant dates will indicate:

■ September 12, 1787—The final draft of the Constitution, written mainly by New York's Gouverneur Morris, was submitted to the Constitutional Convention.

■ October 27, 1787—The first "Federalist" paper appeared in New York City newspapers. The paper was one of a series of eighty-five written by Alexander Hamilton (New York signer of the Constitution), James Madison, and John Jay, who supported adoption of the Constitution and advocated a strong federal government. (Hamilton, a brilliant and courageous statesman, as well as an admittedly difficult and obstinate man, was sharply criticized for his federalist views. His enemies called him a monarchist who wanted to enthrone an American king. Refusing to let the scorn defeat him, Hamilton went on to serve his country with honor and distinction.)

■ July 26, 1788—New York ratified the Constitution, the eleventh state to do so.

■ September 13, 1788—New York City was named the nation's capital, and Federal Hall at Wall and Broad streets became the first national capitol building. New York held this honor until December 6, 1790, when Philadelphia became the temporary capital prior to the permanent move to Washington, D.C.

■ March 4, 1789—The first U.S. Congress met in New York City.

■ April 30, 1789—George Washington was inaugurated as first

▲ Mott Street, with Bayard Street, forms one of the crossroads of Chinatown.

▶ Telephone booths in Chinatown reflect the neighborhood's ethnic heritage.

President of the United States at Federal Hall on Wall Street. "The Father of His Country" was sworn in by Chancellor of New York State Robert Livingston, and the Bible used on that historic day is the same one used by President George Bush at his inauguration on January 20, 1989. After his inauguration ceremonies, President Washington worshipped at St. Paul's Chapel, on Broadway at Fulton Street, and his pew can still be seen. A handsome church, surrounded by a colonial graveyard, St. Paul's was designed by architect Thomas McBean after London's St. Martin-in-the-Fields Church on Trafalgar Square. Federal Hall, where Washington took the oath of office on the balcony looking down Broad Street, has not survived. In its place is a Greek Revival building erected in 1834–42. Originally a custom house, from 1842 to 1862, it then served as a subtreasury building until 1925, when it was designated Federal Hall National Memorial. On the front steps is a heroic 1883 statue of President Washington by J.Q.A. Ward, and inside is a new Museum of American Constitutional Government, which marks the bicentennial of Washington's inauguration.

■ September 22, 1789—Congress established the office of Postmaster General, and Benjamin Franklin became the first to hold the position. Two days later Congress established the U.S. Supreme Court.

■ February 27, 1790—New York became the sixth state to ratify the Bill of Rights (the first ten amendments to the Constitution).

If New York City lost its cachet as capital of the country, it quickly moved to establish itself as the capital of commerce. Alexander Hamilton established the Bank of New York—the first bank in the city and the third in the nation—and the New York Stock Exchange was founded by twenty-four brokers meeting under a buttonwood tree at Wall and William streets in 1792.

Little Old New York was growing. By 1790, when the first census was taken, the population had grown to 33,000, making the city the largest in the nation, and that figure would double by 1800.

Great strides were being made in the field of transportation. In 1807, Robert Fulton demonstrated his *Clermont* steamboat on the Hudson River, where it began regular service between the city and Albany, the new upstate capital. (Fulton, for whom Fulton Street is named, is buried in the graveyard of Trinity Church.) Both the Erie Canal—which opened in 1825 and connected the Great Lakes with the Hudson River, and therefore with the Atlantic Ocean—and the New York & Harlem Railroad, which opened in 1832, greatly increased the city's commerce.

◄ People come from all over to buy the condiments, spices, and exotic sauces that are only available in Chinatown.

▼ Chinatown, New York's most ethnically concentrated neighborhood, is best experienced on a walking tour. Negotiating the crowded sidewalks and streets is part of the fun. Scores of Chinese restaurants and food stalls attract thousands of gourmets each day—many of them lawyers, jurists, and jurors from the city's adjacent court district.

Little Italy *(top and bottom)*, just north of Chinatown across Canal Street, celebrates the Feast of San Gennaro, patron saint of Naples, each September.

►► Lower East Side, around Orchard and Delancey streets, is the New York shopper's bargain basement. Everything from clothes to china, linens to eyeglasses, and toys to jewelry can be found in the stores and sidewalk stalls.

▲ At the turn of the century, pushcarts and vendors selling fruits and vegetables were familiar sights, especially in Greenwich Village and what is now SoHo. Today, only a few remain.

▶▶ Clockwise from top:

The streets of SoHo, once teeming with trucks during the day and deserted at night, have been transformed into New York's newest art colony.

Tenements and town houses still line the streets of SoHo, Greenwich Village, and Chelsea.

This former working man's refuge in SoHo is a now-fashionable corner spot.

By 1840, New York had become the shipbuilding center and largest port in the U.S.A. The recently renovated South Street Seaport, just below the Brooklyn Bridge on Manhattan's East River waterfront, tells the story of the city's seafaring days in a multimedia show called "The Seaport Experience." The Seaport also offers piers with historic ships, beautifully restored eighteenth-century buildings, museum exhibits, and a bevy of shops and restaurants, including two long-established seafood houses, Sweets and Sloppy Louie's.

The biggest setback in the forward march of early nineteenth-century New York was the War of 1812, brought on by Britain's impressment of American seamen, its illegal searching of our ships, and its flagrant interference with the principles of free trade. Although the war never touched New York (the two forts built to guard the harbor, Castle Clinton in Battery Park and its twin on Governors Island, were never used for military purposes), British blockades did interrupt commerce, and business-minded New Yorkers sighed with relief when the peace treaty was signed in Ghent, Belgium, on Christmas Eve, 1814.

Another serious setback of the early nineteenth century was the disastrous fire of 1835, which destroyed most of old Dutch New York. Two results of the tragedy were the establishment of strict building codes (which New York maintains to this day) and

the construction of the Croton Water System (now greatly expanded), which ensured that a plentiful supply of pure water would flow into the city from the hills to the north.

Two pleasant events brightened spirits before the Civil War brought new troubles to the city: the 1853 opening of the first American World's Fair at the glittering Crystal Palace (which stood where Bryant Park is located today) and the 1858 beginning of Central Park, a masterwork of the landscape architects Frederick Law Olmsted and Calvert Vaux.

A MIDWESTERNER CHARMS NEW YORK

The first time Abraham Lincoln came to New York City it was to make his electrifying "right makes might" speech on February 27, 1860, in the brand-new Cooper Union Building on Astor Place. The packed house that paid twenty-five cents each to hear the gawky, ill-at-ease office-seeker from the Midwest was skeptical and derisive at first, but the tall, slender figure, gaining confidence as he warmed to his subject—abolition—soon had the audience mesmerized. So successful was the speech that it is credited with winning Lincoln the presidential nomination.

Cooper Union today (the oldest extant building framed with steel beams in America) is The Cooper Union for the Advancement of Science and Art, and its well-kept Great Hall,

◄◄ Clockwise from top left:

The West Village—the true Greenwich Village, as many residents claim—is a delightful area of early- and late-nineteenth-century town houses.

Bleecker is one of the leading commercial streets of Greenwich Village.

A sidewalk artist at work.

◄ Some of New York's finest jazz artists perform at this long-established club.

▼ Bleecker Street in Greenwich Village.

▼ SoHo *(top)* is famous for its eclectic style. Street fairs and flea markets *(bottom)* are common events in New York throughout the year.

►► Washington Square Park in Greenwich Village.

where Lincoln spoke, is now the scene of various educational and entertainment programs. A stone's throw from Cooper Union at 428-434 Lafayette Street are the last four of nine magnificent 1833 town houses, joined together and sharing an imposing Corinthian colonnade. Across the street is the even more impressive Astor Library (1853–81), now the home of producer Joseph Papp's New York Shakespeare Festival Public Theater, which has turned Astor's reading rooms into a series of splendid Off-Broadway theaters. *A Chorus Line, Hair* and *For Colored Girls . . .* were originally produced here, in addition to highly imaginative presentations of Shakespeare's plays. Nearby, at 15 East 7th Street, is the 1854 McSorley's Old Ale House, where Lincoln supposedly stopped for a draft when he was in the neighborhood.

The body of President Abraham Lincoln lay in state in New York's City Hall on April 24, 1865, while en route by train for burial in Illinois. An estimated 120,000 New Yorkers filed past the bier to mourn their beloved leader.

For New York City the most tragic battle of the Civil War was an internal one. New Yorkers, being business-minded, were largely opposed to the war and made several attempts to prevent it, suggesting compromises. In spite of these efforts, Fort Sumter was fired upon, and the conflict was joined. Although 8,000 patriotic New Yorkers volunteered for the Union forces, the need (300,000 men) was much greater and a draft was imposed in May 1863. One provision of the draft call—well-to-do men could pay $300 and escape service—created such intense resentment that a mob, fired up by agitators, attacked the registration office. This led to three days of violent rioting, by as many as 70,000 men and women, during which millions of dollars worth of property was destroyed and a thousand people were killed. It was one of the most shameful episodes in the city's history.

At the beginning of the Civil War, New York was going through an economic slump, but when the clouds of conflict cleared, the city found itself richer than ever before. (One of the ironic truths about war is that it often brings prosperity to areas removed from the battlefields.) Throughout the war New York had acted as a supply depot, providing both men and money (an estimated half-billion dollars) to the Union forces at the front. Although Manhattan lost population during the war—down almost 100,000 to 730,000—the city's coffers, both public and private, were full. Abundant nourishment was ready and waiting for The Big Apple's eager roots: the postwar prosperity period had begun. By 1870, just five years after the war's end, New York would be known as the wealthiest and most economically influential city in the nation. A boom had been launched, one that has had its ups and downs over the ensuing decades but one that has continued to the present day.

HOW THE APPLE GREW

While pre-Civil War immigration to New York had been sizable, the latter half of the nineteenth century brought the waves of immigrants who gave the city the character and shape we know today. Between 1860 and 1900, the population of Manhattan alone more than doubled—from 813,660 to 1,850,093—and that of the entire city area (the boroughs were separate entities until unification in 1898) almost tripled, going from 1,174,779 to 3,437,202.

Fortunately, the city's rapid growth had been predicted and prepared for by the earliest city fathers. In the 1640s lots were

blocked out along the newly formed streets of lower Manhattan, and in 1811 the city mapped out its rectangular street pattern, or grid plan, that today makes New York one of the easiest of all large cities to navigate. (Two exceptions to the grid pattern are lower Manhattan and Greenwich Village, especially the West Village, where street patterns and property lines had been established before 1811.) Later on, in the twentieth century, other problems of city growth—such as the number, height and density of skyscrapers and the need to distinguish between commercial and residential areas—led to a series of strict and binding building codes, fire prevention regulations, zoning ordinances, landmarking provisions, and city-planning measures. All of this activity led to the formation of such bodies as the Port of New York Authority (1921), the Regional Planning Association (1929), the Municipal Housing Authority (1934), and the City Planning Commission (1938), which oversee and regulate such aspects of the city as housing, bridges, tunnels, highways, and airports.

As the city grew in the latter half of the nineteenth century, it moved steadily and northward along the 1811 grid plan. Lower Manhattan, which had once been both residential and commercial, began losing residents (at least those who could afford to move) to the more fashionable (and, it was thought, more healthful) areas of Greenwich Village (especially around Washington Square) and lower Fifth Avenue. From there, the trendsetters moved into middle Fifth Avenue and areas to the east such as Gramercy Park and Murray Hill. Always restless, always fickle, always moving, society next colonized upper Fifth Avenue (particularly along and overlooking Central Park) and the avenues directly to the east, Madison and Park. As for the Upper West Side, it was definitely a latecomer. When the famous Dakota was built in 1884 as the city's first luxury apartment house, it was the only building on its side of town and was thought to be as far away as the Dakota Territory. (Still one of the most desirable addresses

▲ ► Two statues of George Washington grace the front of Washington Arch; this one was sculpted by A. Sterling Calder, the father of the "mobile" artist, Alexander Calder. The marble arch itself was designed by Stanford White and erected in 1889 to commemorate the 100th anniversary of George Washington's inauguration. Framed by the arch are the Twin Towers of the World Trade Center.

► ► The 1876 Jefferson Market Courthouse has been a branch of the New York Public Library since 1967.

▼ "The Old North Row," a splendid stand of nineteenth-century Greek Revival town houses, is all that remains of the Washington Square that Henry James and Edith Wharton knew.

▲ Artists and photographers are especially fond of this element of the New York City landscape: roof-top water tanks.

(preceding pages) Con Edison clock tower on Irving Place, surrounded by the red, pyramid-shaped towers of the new Zeckendorf apartment house complex at Union Square and 14th Street.

◄ ◄ Clockwise from top:

St. George's Church, facing Stuyvesant Square at East 16th Street. Built in 1856, the famous banker J.P. Morgan was a regular member of its congregation.

O. Henry liked to sit in the front booth of this Gramercy Park area restaurant.

This equestrian statue of George Washington (1856) is now at the entrance to Union Square; originally, it was at Fourth Avenue and 14th Street.

in Manhattan, the Dakota has been home to such luminaries as Lauren Bacall and Yoko Ono, whose husband John Lennon was shot there, in the entranceway, on December 8, 1980.)

It was perhaps perfectly natural for a still-developing, still-unsure-of-itself society to move around this rapidly—to follow the herd—rather than stay put and make a stand, but the quirky nature of the city's growth often made frequent changes of address mandatory. Overnight what had been a quiet residential neighborhood could suddenly turn commercial, as did the Lafayette Street area below Astor Place and the area that is now SoHo. Furthermore, people moved around because they could move around: there was plenty of stretching room in Little Old New York. It's ironic to note that although the city moved steadily northward in the old days, the trend has been reversed in late-twentieth-century Manhattan. Lower Manhattan—in areas such as SoHo, TriBeCa, the South Street Seaport, and that brand-new landfill area called Battery Park City—has acquired a residential population once again, as house- and apartment-hungry young professionals have moved into converted lofts and other commercial properties as well as new co-op and condo towers.

Greenwich Village, always unique, remains the exception in the changing face of New York. Ever since the eighteenth century, when early New Yorkers fled the diseases and miasmas of lower Manhattan for the more salubrious air of the farms and fields

north of Canal Street, Greenwich Village has remained residential, a neighborhood of town houses, small shops, intimate restaurants, Off-Broadway theaters, and schools and institutions of higher learning such as New York University. Now largely landmarked—especially the West and South Village areas—the Village's outward face cannot be changed or altered without the approval of a battery of boards and commissions.

Population growth and the expansion of the city were not the only characteristics of the post-Civil War era in New York. Startling developments and events were taking place in the social, cultural, scientific, political, religious, intellectual, and architectural aspects of city living. The following highlights of the period will indicate what a yeasty time it was in Big Apple history, an astonishingly productive and progressive time when many of the city's most beloved and revered institutions—and many of the modern inventions without which we could not exist today—were added to the city scene.

1870 Grand Central Terminal, often known as Grand Central Station, opens (at 42nd Street and Park Avenue) to a public ready and eager to go places and do things.

1874 The cornerstone of the American Museum of Natural History (now the largest museum in New York City) is laid by President Ulysses S. Grant.

▲ Gramercy Park is not open to the public—only to those area residents who have a key. The surrounding neighborhood is one of the city's most delightful.

▶ This statue of Edwin Booth, the great nineteenth-century actor, is in Gramercy Park, not far from The Players—a private club he established for actors and other notables.

▼ Gramercy Park, which was laid out in 1831, boasts some of the finest landmark houses in the city. Many say it is the part of New York that most resembles London.

1878 The Bell Telephone Company of New York is founded, and the next year the city's first commercial telephone exchange is opened at 82 Nassau Street. The city's first telephone directory? A mere card bearing 252 names!

1879 The new St. Patrick's Cathedral at Fifth Avenue and 50th Street is dedicated on May 25, and the name Madison Square Garden was given to Gilmore's Concert Garden on the square's northeast corner. (There were two Gardens on the original Madison Square site before moves to Eighth Avenue and 50th Street and lastly to its present Penn Station location.)

1880 The Metropolitan Museum of Art's first wing in Central Park at Fifth Avenue and 82nd Street is opened on March 30 by President Rutherford B. Hayes. Sarah Bernhardt makes her American debut at Booth's Theater.

1882 Thomas Alva Edison, at 3 p.m. on September 4, in a "dynamo room" at 257 Pearl Street, signals for the master switch to be pulled. As if by magic, the first homes and offices in New York City to be electrically wired are illuminated—as *The New York Times* said the next day, "with no nauseous smell, no flicker and no glare." The picturesque (but impractical) days of gas lighting were over. Today, New York City takes its electricity for granted—that is, until a massive blackout comes along, as it did in 1965 and 1977.

The Metropolitan Life Insurance Company headquarters looms in the foreground of this skyline scene—a perspective that makes the much taller Empire State Building in the background seem smaller.

1883 The Brooklyn Bridge—the one and only, the mighty and the magnificent—opens on May 24, an everlasting tribute to the courage, stamina, and genius of German engineer John Augustus Roebling. Elaborate fireworks accompany its gala unveiling (as well as its 100th birthday in 1983). In the fall of 1883, on October 22, another New York institution, The Metropolitan Opera, opens on Broadway and 39th Street, winning raves for its acoustics and its artists, if not for its architecture. The opening night opera: *Faust,* starring Christine Nilsson as Margherita. (In 1966, the Met moved to its present location at Lincoln Center.)

1886 The Statue of Liberty, a gift from the people of France to the people of the United States, is dedicated on Bedloes Island (now Liberty Island), in New York harbor on October 28, with President Grover Cleveland in attendance. An amazing, almost incredible structure, Liberty was the brainchild of Prof. Édouard-René Lefebvre de Laboulaye and was sculpted by Frédéric Auguste Bartholdi. The interior framework was the work of Alexandre Gustave Eiffel of Eiffel Tower fame. Formally called "Liberty Enlightening the World," the statue stands

151 feet tall on a pedestal 89 feet high, resting on the 65-foot, star-shaped base of old Fort Wood. (As a National Monument, the Statue of Liberty belongs to the citizens of the United States, so don't be drawn into the old and rather tired argument over whether it is "owned" by New York or New Jersey.) The famous poem "The New Colossus," written by Emma Lazarus in 1883, is now inscribed on the base of the statue. The last five lines are the most frequently quoted:

Give me your tired, your poor,
Your huddled masses yearning to breathe free,
The wretched refuse of your teeming shore.
Send these, the homeless, the tempest-tost to me,
I lift my lamp beside the golden door.

Although Liberty was rededicated on its 100th anniversary, October 28, 1986, the completely restored statue was unveiled the previous July 3, during "Liberty Weekend '86," a glittering schedule of special events that lasted through July 6. The events included an International Naval Review and Operation Sail '86 ("Tall Ships"), a Harbor Festival throughout Lower Manhattan, an American music spectacular, a Central Park classical music concert that drew 800,000 spectators, and two fireworks extravaganzas that attracted millions of viewers. President Ronald Reagan and Vice-President George Bush attended the ceremonies and presided at various events.

1891 Carnegie Hall, a name that evokes fine music—be it symphony, chamber, jazz, pop or whatever—formally opens on May 5, 1891. With Andrew Carnegie, the eponymous benefactor, in his box (#33), conductor Walter Damrosch began the proceedings, and then the great Russian composer Peter Ilyich Tchaikovsky, invited here for the occasion, ascended the podium to conduct his own "Marche Solennelle." Then, as now, the hall was praised for its acoustics.

1892 Ellis Island, a 27½-acre National Monument in New York harbor, opens as New York's immigration station; and before it closes in 1954, some 12 million people from all over the world will be processed here. (All in all, some 17

The Flatiron Building *(these pages)*, built in 1902, was originally known as the Fuller Building, and was among the first of the city's skyscrapers. In Renaissance Revival style, with a rusticated limestone façade, its triangular design was dictated by the site.

60

When snow visits *(top)*, it softens the edges and noise of the city. Holiday lights *(bottom)* are reflected in the light of a New York taxi.

(preceding pages) In recent years, the tops of more and more skyscrapers have been illuminated at night.

►► Macy's is garlanded with lights at Christmastime.

Garfield the Cat, one of the giant balloons in the annual Macy's Thanksgiving Day Parade, is inflated the night before at 77th Street and Central Park West.

million immigrants passed through New York City during the 1892–1954 period, but not all of them were processed on Ellis Island.) As a result of these waves of immigration—from Ireland and Scotland, Italy and Germany, Spain and Eastern Europe, Greece and Turkey, Russia and China—it is estimated that 40 percent of all Americans have Ellis Island roots. Although a few of the immigrants were well-to-do, drawn to America by a sense of adventure, the overwhelming majority were fleeing starvation, unemployment, and religious or political persecution. That's why their first glimpse of the Statue of Liberty was such an emotional experience; here at last was a symbol of freedom and promise.

While most immigrants remembered Ellis Island as a happy experience, full of expectation for a bright future, for some it was a place of dashed hopes. If the examining doctors found a communicable disease—tuberculosis and a virulent eye infection were common maladies at the time—the affected immigrant was refused entrance to the New World. Dreams turned to nightmares as families and loved ones were divided. But if Ellis Island provided a less than ideal welcome to the new arrivals, at least it tried to

process them with as much dignity and efficiency as possible. Earlier, between 1855 and 1890, Castle Garden at the Battery (formerly Castle Clinton, the 1811 fort) was used as the immigration station; before that, immigrants simply were dumped on the docks, where many fell immediate prey to all sorts of scams and exploitations (especially those immigrants who knew little or no English). By the time Ellis Island was established, immigrant aid organizations representing each nationality were on hand to assist the often helpless arrivals.

Today there is a small museum honoring early immigrants at restored Castle Clinton in Battery Park (where you book passage on the Circle Line ferries to the Statue of Liberty) and a much larger Museum of Immigration in the base of the statue. The refurbishing of Ellis Island continues—the Great Hall has already been restored to its 1918–24 appearance.

In addition to Ellis Island, the year 1892 marks the laying of the cornerstone of the Cathedral Church of St. John the Divine, the largest Gothic cathedral in the world. Although not yet completed (work is still proceeding on such areas as the west front towers, the central dome, and

66

▲ Garfield and other balloons float over the parade route on their way downtown.

▼ Macy's Thanksgiving Day Parade draws thousands of spectators.

the north and south transepts), St. John's is very much an active community-involved parish. It can seat 10,000 worshippers. It has a regular schedule of plays, concerts, and art exhibits, and it has been the site of funerals for famous New Yorkers (writer James Baldwin, one of Harlem's most distinguished sons, was buried from St. John's). Visitors are also invited to watch the cathedral builders at work—the master craftsmen and their apprentices, all of whom have been trained in the arts and crafts of stone carving and cutting as practiced in medieval days.

1893 The first theater in the Times Square area (then called Longacre Square) is opened by Charles Frohman at 40th Street and Broadway, just north of the Metropolitan Opera House. "The Great White Way" is born!

1897 The first Waldorf-Astoria Hotel (a combination of the 1893 Waldorf and the new adjacent Astoria) opens on Fifth Avenue on what is now the site of the Empire State Building, and tourism—today the city's fastest-growing industry—takes a giant leap into the future.

BENEATH THE SURFACE OF THE GILDED AGE

The remarkable advances made by New York City from 1865 to the turn of the century—in science, industry, and the arts—should not blind anyone to the adversities, the inequities, the sufferings (both physical and mental) that festered beneath the veneer of the Gilded Age.

Otto L. Bettmann of the Bettmann Archive, in his provocatively titled book *The Good Old Days—They Were Terrible!*, seeks to dispel the "benevolent haze," the rosy nostalgia, that has tended to cloud a true picture of the times:

The good old days were good for but the privileged few. For the farmer, the laborer, the average bread-winner, life was an unremitting hardship. This segment of the population was exploited or lived in the shadow of total neglect. And youth had no voice. . . . I have always felt that our times have over-rated and unduly overplayed the fun aspects of the past. What we have forgotten are the hunger of the unemployed, crime, corruption, the despair of the aged, the insane and the crippled.

Lithographs, cartoons, and photographs of the period are graphic proof of Bettmann's words. They depict polluted air, thick with industrial smoke . . . garbage-strewn streets . . . highways and byways clogged with horsedrawn wagons and carriages . . . unspeakable slums and tenement apartments crammed with human misery . . . intolerable sweatshop working conditions . . . unsanitary conditions leading to tainted food and drink . . . and rampant street crime, prostitution, gambling, private and governmental graft and judicial corruption.

Undoubtedly the most notorious criminal to stride across the era, a man whose name has become synonymous with political sin, was William Marcy "Boss" Tweed. An enormous man with gargantuan appetites, Tweed probably swindled New York City and its taxpayers out of a total $200 million, a considerable fortune in the 1860s and '70s. As historian Edward Robb Ellis has written in his narrative history, *The Epic of New York:*

He was the first city politician in the United States to be called the Boss. He enslaved New York City and the state of New York, and he planned to put America into one of

▲ Snoopy—the float—has had three incarnations. His first appearance was in 1968; his second was in 1985, after a two-year retirement. This latest appearance with Woodstock began in 1987.

▼ Ronald McDonald is a favorite with the young set.

The Empire State Building is one of the most famous skyscrapers in the world.

► A glistening limestone-and-steel marvel, the Empire State Building welcomes 2 million visitors a year to its observation decks on the 86th and 102nd floors.

◄ ◄ Two remarkable skyscrapers: the sleek and graceful Chrysler Building (*foreground*) and the majestic Empire State Building.

▼ The lobby of the Empire State Building is notable for its Art Deco wall decorations. There are also fanciful panels illustrating the wonders of the ancient world.

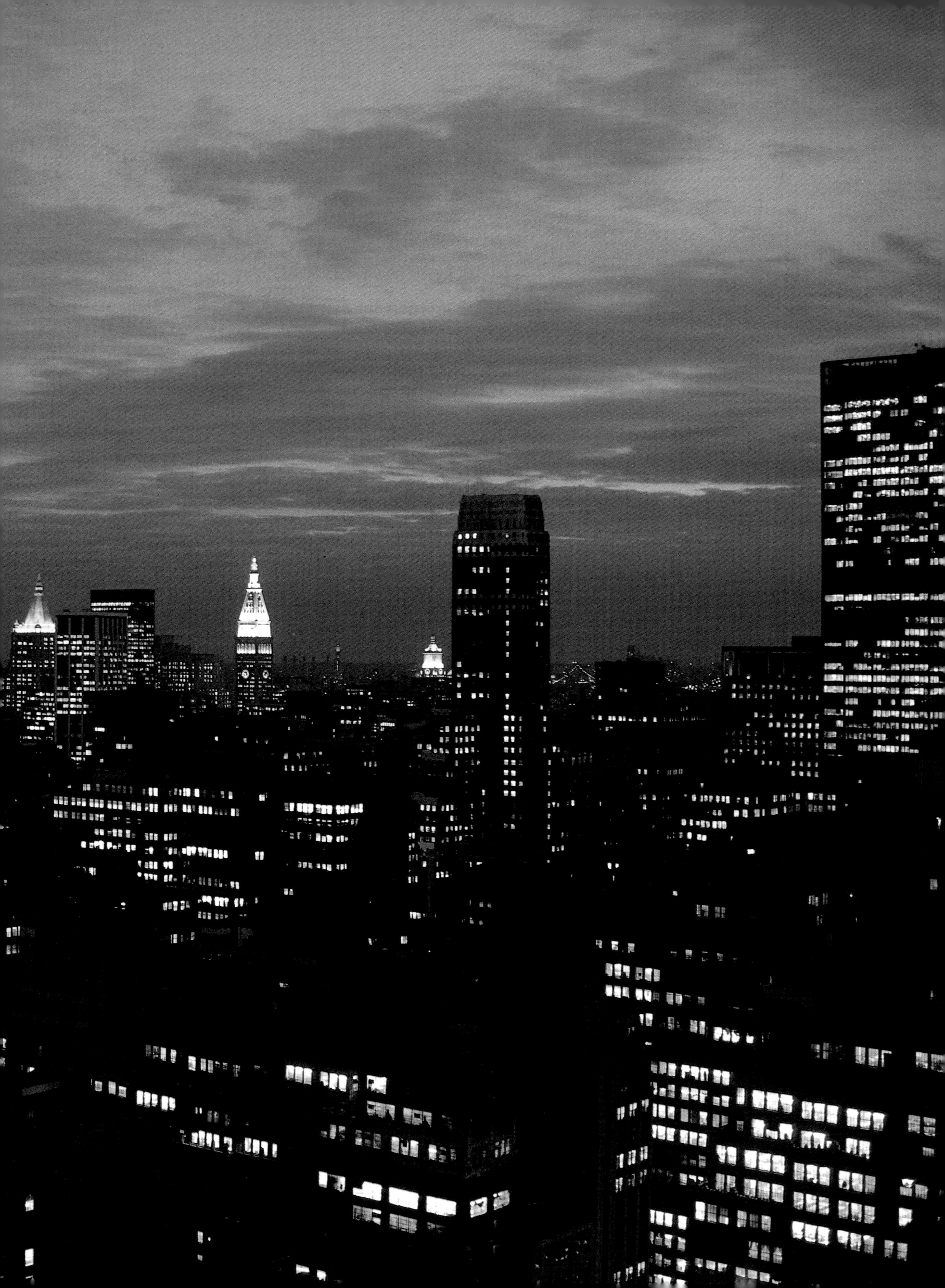

his huge pockets. Tweed became the third largest property owner in the city, lived in baronial splendor in a Fifth Avenue mansion, and kept a country house, whose mahogany stables were trimmed in silver. Devoid of religious faith, he believed in just two things—himself and power.

Over a political career of almost thirty years, Tweed rigged elections, bribed government officials, controlled government purse strings, dominated government boards, set up the Tweed Ring that extended his authority over all branches of the city administration, took control of Tammany Hall (which controlled the Democratic Party in a predominantly Democratic city), bought the silence of most newspapers, railroaded legislation, stifled personal initiative and business development (if they ran counter to his plans), schemed to corner the gold market, and constantly, unceasingly, dipped into any till he could find. He justified his flagrant behavior by saying, "The fact is that New York politics were always dishonest—long before my time."

Tweed's inevitable downfall came when he grew careless and overly confident, and his cronies—demanding ever-bigger slices of the pie—turned on him. Two of them took their inside stories (backed up by copies of official records) to the *Times,* and the end of Boss Tweed's reign began. After two trials (Tweed's

(preceding pages) The city at night, looking southwest.

► The Jacob K. Javits Convention Center was designed by I. M. Pei. Many people, including architectural critics, think it is the most beautiful, most distinctive convention center in the world.

▼ Chelsea's slick and sassy Empire Diner never closes.

▲ The Jacob K. Javits Convention Center has been nicknamed The Crystal Palace.

▼ Once the *Intrepid* defended America's freedom in war zones around the world; now the aircraft carrier has been converted to the Intrepid Sea-Air-Space Museum and is moored in the Hudson at West 46th Street.

(following pages) New York's crowded cityscape.

▲ Not all of the attractions in Rockefeller Center are buildings.

◀ The Guardian Angels are volunteer crime-fighters.

lawyers probably packed the hung jury during the first one), the Boss was sentenced to twelve years in prison and fined $12,750 (reduced on appeal to one year and $250). After his release, he was rearrested, slapped with a huge new civil suit, and imprisoned once again because he couldn't make the $3 million bail; he escaped (during one of his permitted afternoon strolls), fled to New Jersey and then to Staten Island, sailed for Florida (where he hid out in the Everglades for a while), moved on to Cuba and finally Spain, where he was apprehended and brought back to Ludlow Street Jail. There he died of pneumonia on April 12, 1878.

Tweed did leave behind something more tangible than a trail of graft and greed. The Old New York Courthouse, the "Tweed Courthouse," still stands behind City Hall on Chambers Street, and it is worth a visit for the peek it gives into a tarnished chapter of city history. During its construction, the Tweed Ring supposedly pocketed $10 million of its total $14 million cost; nevertheless, the $4 million spent produced a notable example of Victorian architecture. Now a landmark, the building looks rather shabby on the outside, but the inner atrium—with its noble staircases, surrounding balconies, and overhead skylight—is certainly impressive.

After Tweed, the other tragedy to hit New York during the so-called Gilded Age was the ferocious Blizzard of 1888. As so often happens in a city noted for its quirky climate, the storm took New Yorkers by surprise, creeping in early on the Monday morning of March 12, when winter should have lost its legs. After what had been a relatively mild winter, the city awoke to a new work week to find that the temperature had plunged to the low 20s, a snowstorm was raging, and drifts—blown by the fierce wind—were piling up in snowbanks 30 feet high. Most businesses closed (or never opened), schools were deserted, the port closed down and traffic—by man, beast, and machine—came to a halt. One newspaper described the storm as if reporting the end of the world: "A horror of darkness deepened on the crowded city and the terror-stricken population cowered at the awful sounds which came from the throat of the whirlwind. . . . It seemed as if a million devils were loose in the air."

By early afternoon, the temperature had dropped to 10 degrees and the wind had increased to 85 miles an hour. That night the temperature sank to almost zero. Before relief came on Tuesday morning, the city had suffered scores of deaths and more than $20 million in property damage in what has been recorded as "the most famous blizzard in American history."

Nothing, however, subdues New York for very long. Recovering from the plague of Boss Tweed and the Blizzard of '88, the city moved into the Gay Nineties with renewed vigor, determined to have a ball before the twentieth century dawned. Mrs. William Astor, whose firm foundation was a fortune estimated at $50 million, was the queen of society, and she regularly entertained its members at her Fifth Avenue mansion. "The Four Hundreds," the term for the crème de la crème of society, stems from the report (again, probably apocryphal, but it makes an amusing story) that only four hundred guests could fit comfortably in Mrs. Astor's ballroom. Besides, claimed social arbiters of the day, there were only four hundred people worth inviting. Among those chosen few were assorted Belmonts,

◄ ◄ Trees in the foreground *(top)* can't compete with this forest of skyscrapers. A marble temple of knowledge, the New York Public Library *(bottom)* at 42nd Street and Fifth Avenue stands on the site of a reservoir that was demolished in 1899. Many consider the building to be the finest example of the Beaux Arts style in the United States.

◄ The library lions represent patience and fortitude.

▼ This figure, representing beauty and inspiration, was placed in its position in 1913.

▲ The United Nations site, a green and gracious stretch along Manhattan's East River, was once a slum area of shanties and slaughterhouses.

(preceding pages) Forty-second Street is one of the New York's busiest thoroughfares.

▼ This sculpture of a man beating his sword into a plowshare—particularly appropriate for an organization fostering world peace—is in the U.N.'s riverfront gardens.

▲ Presidents and potentates, dictators and demagogues, men and women of peace address the U.N.'s General Assembly, and the world listens.

▼ Flags of all the member nations flutter in front of the U.N. General Assembly Building.

Flaglers, Rockefellers, Vanderbilts, and Whitneys—all captains of industry in an increasingly prosperous city. By day they worked at building up the fortunes that would later be used to erect some of the city's most enduring monuments and to endow and support many of our museums, schools, hospitals, charities, theaters, religious landmarks, and institutions of higher learning, but at night they relaxed and enjoyed themselves.

Another layer of New York society—perhaps not as fashionable but probably a lot more fun—was composed of the city's actors, writers, entertainers, sports figures, and assorted bons vivants—names like Lillian Russell, "Diamond Jim" Brady, Mark Twain, Lily Langtry, and John L. Sullivan, the noted boxer. They used to congregate in such plush palaces as the Murray Hill Hotel and the Broadway Central Hotel; they ate enormous and endless meals at Delmonico's, Luchow's, and Cavanaugh's; they shopped at Siegel-Cooper (the magnificent building is still standing at Sixth Avenue and 18th Street) and other "Ladies' Mile" stores; they were regular patrons at the theaters around Union Square; and they gambled and attended sporting events at popular Long Island spas and pleasure spots like Coney Island and Sheepshead Bay in Brooklyn.

Capping an era was a most significant event in New York's political history: the consolidation of all five boroughs—Brooklyn (or Kings County, as it was then called), Queens, Manhattan, Staten Island (Richmond) and The Bronx—into Greater New York on January 1, 1898. The result was truly The Big Apple, a metropolis of more than 3 million people—the largest city in the world.

NEW YORK THRILLS TO THE 20TH CENTURY

With the turning of the last century, Little Old New York became history in more ways than one. As if to prove that "the Twentieth Century" really was as portentous as it sounded, the city embarked on a building boom that would radically change its profile and give new meaning to the word *skyline*. The dawning of a new era had put New Yorkers in an optimistic mood; everyone was looking up, and the city was reaching for the sky. The Age of Skyscrapers was born.

Some historians claim that New York's first skyscraper was Cyrus W. Field's twelve-story Washington Building, a solid masonry structure built in 1882 at 1 Broadway. Margot Gayle, an authority on cast-iron architecture and the person credited with saving the Cast-Iron District (or SoHo, as it is now called, for *south* of *Houston*), might argue that the handsome, prefab facades of late-nineteenth-century cast-iron buildings, which could be selected by style from an ironworks' catalog, were the precursors of skyscrapers. Historian Edward Robb Ellis holds that only a steel-skeleton building can be called a true skyscraper. He claims that the city's first *real* skyscraper was the thirteen-story Tower Building at 50 Broadway.

In any case, the direction was set: the future growth of the city was up, up, up. Two factors made this trend advantageous and possible. First, Manhattan Island is long (13.4 miles) and

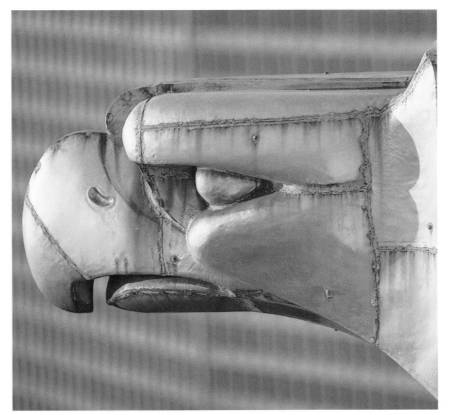

▲ A gargoyle modeled after a hood ornament guards one of the setbacks on the Chrysler Building.

◄ No New York skyscraper has a more graceful spire than that of the Chrysler Building.

◄◄ Fashionable Upper East Side apartment houses face the East River and the morning sun.

◀ ◀ Original lighting design for the Chrysler Building's spire, long out of use, once again enhances the nighttime skyline.

◀ White neon tubing outlines the triangles within the Chrysler Building's scalloped spire.

▼ "Transportation" is the title of the limestone sculpture group atop the main entrance to Grand Central Terminal *(top)*. Jules Coutan completed the work in 1912. "Transportation" and the Chrysler Building *(bottom)* are two architectural highlights of New York.

▼ "Meet me at the clock in Grand Central"—the start of many a pleasant evening in the city (top). Main concourse of Grand Central Terminal (bottom). At 275 feet long, 120 feet wide, and 125 feet high, it is one of the world's great public spaces.

►► The Pan Am Building is Grand Central's gigantic neighbor on 45th Street.

comparatively narrow (2.3 miles at its widest point); future expansion had to be concentrated, not spread out. Second, the underlying foundation of the island is Manhattan schist, an extremely dense and durable rock that can support buildings of enormous weight and extreme height.

The eccentric but graceful twenty-one-story Flatiron Building at Broadway and 23rd Street (1902) and the neo-Gothic, sixty-story Woolworth Building at Broadway and Park Place (1913), both still standing, were among the first skyscrapers to dazzle the world. They paved the way for those wonders to come: the seventy-seven-story Chrysler Building (1930), the seventy-story RCA Building, now called the GE Building (1931), the 102-story Empire State Building (1931) and the 110-story Twin Towers of the World Trade Center (1962).

As the turn-of-the century city was physically going through the roof, its businessmen were doing the same. In 1900, banker J. Pierpont Morgan established the U.S. Steel Company, the nation's first billion-dollar corporation, and Andrew Carnegie, the industrialist, was doing so well that in 1901 he donated more than sixty libraries to neighborhoods throughout the city. One by one the new New York millionaires began building mansions for themselves, generally along upper Fifth Avenue facing Central Park: Philip Lehman at 7 West 54th Street (1900), Andrew Carnegie at 2 East 91st Street (1901), Felix M. Warburg at Fifth and 92nd Street (1908), and Henry Clay Frick at 1 East 70th Street (1914). J. P. Morgan, always the individualist, decided to take root in Murray Hill, at 33 East 36th Street, in 1906. All of these fine houses are still standing, and most have been converted into museums. The Carnegie home is now the Cooper-Hewitt Museum, the Smithsonian Institution's National

▲ St. Bartholomew's Church on Park Avenue, long a favored venue for society and celebrity weddings.

◀ The Waldorf-Astoria—the very name of which connotes the zenith of hotel class and comfort. U.N. ambassadors have lived here, presidents have stayed here, Cole Porter once had a suite (his piano is now in Peacock Alley), and celebrities by the dozens call it home away from home.

▶ Park Avenue is now commercial in the forties, but its upper reaches still boast some of the most exclusive apartment houses in town.

▼ Spire of the Helmsley Building overlooking Park Avenue.

Museum of Design. The Warburg house has become the Jewish Museum. The Frick mansion contains the owner's incredibly rich collection of paintings, sculpture and furnishings. Its glories include a room filled with decorative panels painted by Fragonard and commissioned by Madame du Barry, El Greco's *St. Jerome,* Rembrandt's *The Polish Rider,* Goya's *The Forge,* and *The Education of the Virgin* by Georges de la Tour.

The Lehman house is not open to the public, but many of its interiors, furnishings, and works of art have been moved to the Lehman Wing of the Metropolitan Museum of Art. As for the J. P. Morgan residence (now the Pierpont Morgan Library), the American Institute of Architects calls it "notable not only for its exhibits of rare prints and manuscripts, but for Morgan's opulent private library, maintained just as he left it."

One of the world's leading research institutions is located on Fifth Avenue between 40th and 42nd Streets. The Main Branch of the New York Public Library, an elegant Beaux Arts building (1911), houses a collection of some 6 million volumes and 17 million documents. The grand-scale entrance hall is the site of changing exhibitions from the library's collection, which also includes prints, drawings, and maps.

An undoubted boost to business in America was the Republican presidency of New Yorker Theodore (Teddy) Roosevelt, who succeeded the assassinated William McKinley in 1901 (the same year of Queen Victoria's death and the coronation of Edward VII). Teddy was bully on business and bully on America, an ideal leader for a nation straining at the leash and raring to go. Today, Theodore Roosevelt's Birthplace—a handsome replica of the Victorian brownstone where the nation's twenty-sixth president lived until he was fourteen—is open to the public at 28 East 20th Street, just west of the attractive Gramercy Park area.

▲ The stars and stripes . . . and stripes.

◀ ITT's Park Avenue headquarters is a prime example of the mirror-wall style.

▲ Snow is often an inconvenience for those travelling by mass transit.

◄ Pedestrians walk carefully during a snowstorm.

Four of the most memorable events of the early 1900s occurred underground, in the East River, on a roof garden, and in a Greenwich Village sweatshop.

In 1904, New York City's first subway line opened, connecting upper and lower Manhattan on the West Side. On October 27, the first train pulled out of the City Hall station in lower Manhattan, headed up to Grand Central Terminal, crossed east to west on the shuttle tracks to Times Square, and from there ran up the West Side to 145th Street. More than 150,000 rode that first day, and the fare was a nickel! This revolutionary development in rapid (and inexpensive) transit gave New Yorkers more mobility than they had ever before enjoyed. It meant that no longer would labor be forced to live relatively close to the job, and the advent of the subway is the principal reason the city's rapidly increasing Black population, migrating here from the Deep South, was able to seek housing in the Harlem area, which up to this time had been a collection of largely German, Irish, Italian, and Jewish neighborhoods.

The second event, a great disaster, occurred on the morning of Wednesday, June 15, 1904, when the *General Slocum,* an excursion boat, left its pier at the foot of East 3rd Street and steamed up the East River bound for Locust Grove on Long Island Sound. Jammed aboard the side-wheeler's three decks

were 1,400 women and children, all German-Americans from the city's Lower East Side and all members of St. Mark's Lutheran Church on East 6th Street. This bright, warm day seemed ideal for their annual Sunday school picnic. Suddenly, when the boat had reached the vicinity of 125th Street, a fire broke out on the main deck. Instead of immediately turning toward land, the captain increased speed in an effort to reach North Brother Island in The Bronx. The ensuing breeze whipped up by this foolish maneuver fanned the flames until the vessel was soon a raging inferno, and panic as well as fire swept the decks. The *General Slocum* finally reached North Brother Island, but by that time it was a doomed ship. The estimated death toll: over 1,000. Today, in the northern part of Tompkins Square in the East Village section of the Lower East Side, there is a memorial fountain erected on May 30, 1905; it depicts a young boy and girl and contains this poignant tribute to the victims: "They were earth's purest children, loving and fair."

The third memorable event was a scandal that took place in 1906 on the night of June 25. Stanford White, the noted and highly successful architect, was watching the show on the roof garden of Madison Square Garden, a building he had designed. Also in attendance that evening was a hot-headed, intensely jealous young wastrel named Harry K. Thaw, whose wife Evelyn Nesbitt,

The impressive entranceway to 30 Rockefeller Plaza.

A.

B.

G.

C.

F.

D.

A. Limestone panels decorating the buildings of Rockefeller Center make this midtown landmark an outdoor art gallery.

B. A golden Mercury, the god of commerce, a fitting emblem at the Channel Gardens entrance to Rockefeller Center.

C. By Lee Lawrie, a subtle low relief of St. Francis of Assisi, his halo formed by the birds he is feeding.

D. "The Joy of Life," a limestone panel by Attilio Piccirilli in Rockefeller Center, shows a youth holding aloft a bunch of grapes, the symbol of joy.

E.

E. Three metal and enamel plaques by Hildreth Meiere—"Song," "Theater," and "Dance"—decorate the 50th Street façade of Radio City Music Hall. This plaque represents "Theater."

F. Fine art throughout Rockefeller Center, regularly cleaned and kept in repair by maintenance crews, make a self-guided walking tour a constant surprise.

G. Above the entrance to 30 Rockefeller Plaza is Lee Lawrie's massive figure of "Genius" and an unusual panel of molded glass segments.

"Atlas," Lee Lawrie's 14,000-pound, 15-foot bronze statue, upholds the world at the entrance to Rockefeller Center's International Building on Fifth Avenue. Defeated by Zeus, Atlas was forced to bear the weight of the world upon his shoulders.

One of the world's most recognizable landmarks: the main entrance to Rockefeller Center with a golden statue of Prometheus.

▲ The Channel Gardens *(left)* leading to the Lower Plaza welcome hundreds of thousands of visitors to Rockefeller Center each holiday season. Sculpted wire angels by Valerie Clarebout *(right)* trumpet the joys of the holiday season at the Channel Gardens.

(preceding pages) Christmas in Rockefeller Center means skaters on the Lower Plaza's rink, with a huge, brightly lighted tree presiding.

▼ The Rockettes, Radio City Music Hall's internationally famous precision-dancers, perform a Christmas-season favorite, "The March of the Wooden Soldiers."

a showgirl, had reportedly been seduced by White before her marriage. On his way out of the roof garden, Thaw stopped by White's table and shot him dead with a pistol. Thaw was later judged insane, a verdict few doubted. Evelyn went on to fame.

The fourth event was the Triangle Shirtwaist Company fire on March 25, 1911, in a ten-story loft building at 22 Washington Place, just off Washington Square in Greenwich Village. Like many factories at the time, this was a sweatshop where young women were virtually locked in and chained to their sewing machines; it had no sprinkler system. The fire broke out at quitting time and, fed by an ankle-deep litter of garment scraps, it became a holocaust in seconds. Firemen were quick to respond but could do little: extension ladders reached only to the sixth floor and water from hoses reached only to the seventh floor. Faced with barred doors, blocked exits, and intense heat, the working girls began jumping.

In little more than ten minutes, more than 140 lost their lives.

As is usually the case, it takes a tragedy to initiate reforms. Following the Triangle fire (now memorialized by a plaque on the building site), the state's labor code was rewritten, and labor unions began their ascendency.

On a happier front, the arts flourished in New York City during the first decades of the twentieth century. In many cases,

performing artists were aided by the technical advances of the day; for example, electric lighting was revolutionizing the theater (previously dependent on gas lighting), and in 1902 Enrico Caruso (perhaps the most famous opera singer of all time) made his first gramophone recording. Over at the Union Square Biograph Studios, 11 East 14th Street, D. W. Griffith directed his first film, *The Adventures of Dollie,* in 1908—an accomplishment made possible by the pioneer work of Thomas Edison, who, on April 23, 1896, unveiled his Vitascope moving images in the Koster and Bials Music Hall, now the site of Macy's department store on West 34th Street. There is a proper plaque on the Macy's site; but, as Richard Alleman points out in his fine book, *The Movie Lover's Guide to New York,* there is none at the Biograph site on 14th Street or at Biograph's original studio site at 841 Broadway. Although Griffith died in 1948, some of his brightest stars lived on for decades; in 1987 his most famous leading lady, New York resident Lillian Gish, starred in the film *The Whales of August.*

In the world of popular music, Irving Berlin, an immigrant lad born in Russia and brought up on the Lower East Side, published his first big hit, "Alexander's Ragtime Band," in 1911, and by the time he died, in 1989 at age 101, in his East Side town house at 17 Beekman Place, he had become America's Music Man. In the

Paul Manship's statue of Prometheus shows the Greek god bringing the gift of fire to mankind.

▲ "New" Rockefeller Center includes the soaring monolithic structures that rose along the Avenue of the Americas in the 1960s and '70s: the Time-Life, Exxon, McGraw-Hill, and Celanese buildings.

(preceding pages) Radio City Music Hall's magnificent Art Deco entranceway on the Avenue of the Americas at 50th Street.

▼ Architectural grandeur is reflected in Rockefeller Center.

world of art, the big news was the "shocking" Armory Show of 1913, which introduced Marcel Duchamp and other European artists as well as the Americans William Blackens, Everett Shinn, and other painters of "The Eight" to New York.

The theater has played a role in New York's cultural life almost from the beginning of the city's history. Before 1900, local stages naturally were dominated by the classics of world drama, foreign imports, and talented (but forgettable) homegrown amateurs. The true geniuses of the American stage had yet to emerge. In addition to standards such as Edmond Rostand's *Cyrano de Bergerac,* William Gillette's *Sherlock Holmes,* James M. Barrie's *The Little Minister* and frequent productions of the plays of Shakespeare and Molière, pre-1900 audiences were given such crowd-pleasers as William Young's *The Rajah, or Wyncot's Ward,* described as "light summer fare" by theater historian Stanley Appelbaum, or Lottie Blair Parker's *Way Down East,* which concerns a once-homeless servant girl who is deceived into a mock marriage—and illegitimate motherhood—by a wealthy villain. After 1900, things picked up a bit with the arrival of plays like Clyde Fitch's *Captain Jinks of the Horse Marines,* a comedy that made Ethel Barrymore a star, James M. Barrie's *Peter Pan,* with the unforgettable Maude Adams and theatrical impresario David Belasco's *The Girl of the Golden West,* which was later used as the basis of Puccini's opera, *La Fanciulla del West.* But it was not until February 2, 1920, that Eugene O'Neill, who is considered by many critics to be America's greatest playwright, arrived on Broadway. His debut on The Great White Way took place at the Morosco Theater, and the play was *Beyond the Horizon,* which won the Pulitzer Prize for that year. The Marriott Marquis Hotel in Times Square now occupies the Morosco site.

War years in a major port city like New York are tense and

▲ Roy Lichtenstein's monumental mural greets visitors to the Equitable Center's soaring, atrium-style lobby.

▼ Equitable Center at Seventh Avenue and 51st Street is a complex that contains fine restaurants, parks, and plazas, stunning art works, and a branch of the Whitney Museum.

trying times. In addition to the ever-present danger of enemy attack, there are the hardships and frustrations imposed upon millions of people packed into an area dependent in large part on supplies from the outside and on the continued movement of its manufactured goods to other parts of the world. Although the United States was actively involved in World War I only for the 1917–18 period, the city was, of course, a focal point for world meetings, business deals, and military preparations throughout the 1914–18 period of conflict. During the active American involvement, troops were constantly passing through on their way to or from the front lines in Europe, hotels were always jammed with those involved in the war in one way or another, and Hollywood stars and local celebrities conducted one Liberty Bond drive after another. Who can forget the old photographs of stars like Douglas Fairbanks, Mary Pickford, and Charlie Chaplin standing on flatbed trucks and giving their all for the war effort?

The cessation of hostilities and the announcement of the armistice on November 11, 1918, was indeed joyous news, but New York's—and the nation's—celebrations were muted by the grim homefront situation. The great influenza epidemic of that year had killed 12,500 New Yorkers (out of a nationwide total of 500,000 and a worldwide total of 21 million). It was the worst plague in the city's history, and the insurance companies paid more money to flu victim beneficiaries than they did to the survivors of World War I soldiers killed in battle.

Locally, the most positive and most encouraging event on the immediate postwar legislative scene was a New York State proposal that led to the passage of the 19th Amendment to the U.S. Constitution: women got the right to vote.

THE '20s ROAR!

After a prolonged struggle as painful as a world war, who wouldn't be ready for a party? Certainly New York City was, and it wasted no time in banishing the blues and striking up the jazz bands.

As if to throw a wet blanket on any postwar fun, the U.S. Congress had passed the 18th Amendment in 1919, and Prohibition shut down bars across the nation. That didn't stop ingenious New York, not for a minute. Overnight, "speakeasies" sprouted like mushrooms in dank basements and back alleys, and each had a heavily guarded door with a small sliding window through which passwords were whispered: "Charlie sent me!" or some such secret saying that would distinguish friends from John Law. Once inside, customers could name their poison: anything from "bathtub gin" to fine Scotch and Canadian whiskeys, depending upon the plushness of the place and the connections of the speak's bootlegger. Some of the joints were lavish nightclubs with top entertainers and floor shows, like Texas Guinan's, whose proprietor sat on the bar, crossed her legs, and greeted incoming patrons with "Hello, suckers!" Vestiges of the speakeasy days can be seen in today's New York but you have to look closely for them; most of the illegal bars—many of them in

(preceding pages) A stainless-steel portion of "Sun Triangle" by Athelstan Spilhaus juts up in front of Rockefeller Center's McGraw-Hill Building.

◄ ▼ St. Patrick's Cathedral, an 1879 reminder of an earlier New York, is a serene presence on Fifth Avenue. For its 100th birthday, the cathedral was cleaned inside and out, revealing details, textures, and stone colors long forgotten. The Cardinal reviews the St. Patrick's Day Parade from the steps of the cathedral.

the West Side theater district—came down with the crumbling brownstones that sheltered them. The world-famous "21" Club at 21 West 52nd Street, once a "speak" and now an exclusive bar and restaurant, is still going strong—as is the place where it started: McBell's bar and restaurant in Greenwich Village on Sixth Avenue near West 4th Street. Also in the Village is Chumley's bar and restaurant, but don't look for a sign because there is none: just find the address at 86 Bedford Street. You no longer have to whisper at Chumley's front door, but the back door "escape hatch" is still available if trouble develops in the front room. Chumley's used to be quite the literary hangout— you'll see all the book jackets prominently displayed—but old timers bitterly remark that they'll let anyone in today.

The arts flourished in the '20s, as did everything else, even though it was a hard time on the artists (too many temptations, too many diversions). Ernest Hemingway and F. Scott Fitzgerald (when they weren't in Paris) cut a wide swath through town. Hemingway hated New York (or so he said), but Fitzgerald ate (and drank) it up; he and his lovely wife Zelda hit every party given and knew every nightspot in town, from the dives down in the Village to the clubs of Harlem. They even spent their honeymoon in New York—in Room 2109 of the now demolished Biltmore Hotel—and Zelda took some highly publicized dips in the Pulitzer Fountain in front of the Plaza Hotel.

In many ways, Fitzgerald was the quintessential New York writer, and he preserved his passion for the city in such novels as *This Side of Paradise* and *The Great Gatsby*. In their charming book, *Literary New York,* Susan Edmiston and Linda D. Cirino quote director Alfred Kazin: "To this day, Fitzgerald remains the only poet of New York's upper-class landmarks. . . . New York was a dreamland to Fitzgerald. It represented his imagination of what is forever charming, touched by the glamour of money, romantically tender and gay."

Although writers lived all over New York during the '20s (Shalom Aleichem, Herman Wouk, and playwright Clifford Odets all lived in The Bronx), the hotbeds of literary fever were Greenwich Village (*the* creative fountainhead), Gramercy Park, Chelsea, the Upper West Side, and Harlem, which, in the '20s, went through a remarkably fertile literary period known as the Harlem Renaissance, when Langston Hughes, Countee Cullen, Zora Neale Hurston, Jean Toomer, Nella Larsen, Arna Bontemps, and Alain Locke (considered to be the father of the Renaissance) were all in full bloom. Among the Villagers were Edna St. Vincent Millay, who wrote romantic verse at 139 Waverly Place, 75½ Bedford Street, "the narrowest house in the Village," and 25 Charlton Street, among numerous addresses; poet Elinor Wylie, who also moved around a lot (1 University Place, 142 East 18th Street, 36 West 9th Street); e. e. cummings, America's lower-case poet, who lived at 4 Patchin Place; Thomas Wolfe, whose 263 West 11th Street digs were described in *You Can't Go Home Again;* and, of course, Eugene O'Neill, a native New Yorker, born in a long-gone Times Square hotel, who despised the city but nevertheless spent a great deal of time in it, generating master-pieces like *The Iceman Cometh, Anna Christie,* for which he won his second Pulitzer in 1922, and *Strange Interlude,* which earned yet another Pulitzer in 1928. O'Neill's early plays—one-act dramas before his full-length Broadway debut with *Beyond the Horizon*—were produced at The Provincetown Playhouse, 133 MacDougal Street, a theatrical shrine that is now home to the camp classics of Charles Busch.

Pulitzer Prizes came thick and fast to the writers working in New York during this heady, intoxicating time. Edith Wharton, the personification of a proper, well-born Manhattan socialite, won hers for a fine novel, *The Age of Innocence* (1921), and Sinclair Lewis, the heart and soul of Middle America, was honored for his novel *Arrowsmith* (1926). Playwright George Kelly won a Pulitzer for *Craig's Wife* (1926), Elmer Rice won for his urban drama *Street Scene* (1929), and Marc Connelly was honored for *The Green Pastures* (1930), which was notable for its all-Black cast.

In midtown, the 1920s' most sacred literary shrine—and one that is active to this day—was the Algonquin Hotel and, specifically, its Rose Room, where the Round Table was located. Here for lunch each day (and sometimes for dinner and later) gathered the sharpest wits of the day, whose every *bon mot* was picked up by the popular press and sent around the world. The Round Table began at about the same time as *The New Yorker* magazine, which was founded by Harold Ross in 1925, and the literary weekly's editors and writers were regulars. Among them were Robert Benchley, Dorothy Parker, *New York Times* drama critic Alexander Woollcott, Edna Ferber, Franklin P. Adams, George S. Kaufman and Marc Connelly. Today, the Algonquin is, as ever, a favorite with visiting writers, directors, producers, actors, and other entertainers. Its Rose Room is a pleasant spot for lunch or dinner, top performers appear in the Oak Room's dinner-cabaret schedule, and the lobby—which hasn't changed since the '20s—is still one of the most comfortable meeting spots and cocktail lounges in town.

Artists found New York a fertile landscape during the '20s and rushed to capture it on canvas. In Greenwich Village at 14-15 Washington Mews, just north of Washington Square, Edward Hopper, William Glackens, and Rockwell Kent all had their studios, turning out unmistakably American paintings and prints that would later enrich the collections of such museums as the Whitney on Madison Avenue and 75th Street. Other artists working in New York at the time were realists George Bellows, John Sloan, and Reginald Marsh; Georgia O'Keeffe, who painted Manhattan skylines and skyscrapers before moving west to paint deserts, rocks, and flowers in her distinctly abstract way; and Alexander Calder, whose mobiles have enhanced the world. (Alexander's father, Sterling Calder, was also an artist; he sculpted one of the statues of George Washington at the Washington Square Arch, the one to the right as you face the Arch looking south.)

What would the Roaring '20s be without their personalities? Babe Ruth, "the Sultan of Swat," was the pride of baseball, as well as the Yankees, and he became home run king in 1927 when he racked up sixty homers in one season. Other sports heroes of the decade included Jack Dempsey, the heavyweight champion, and Bobby Jones, the champion golfer.

On May 20, 1927, Charles Augustus "Lucky Lindy" Lindbergh took off from Roosevelt Field, Long Island, in his Wright-powered Ryan monoplane, *The Spirit of St. Louis,* to make the first solo transatlantic flight. He stayed aloft and awake for the entire 3,600-mile flight to Le Bourget Field in Paris, and his flying time was 33 hours and 39 minutes. Huge crowds on both sides of the ocean were delirious. Also making history that year, but in a different field, was stage star Al Jolson, whose movie, *The Jazz Singer,* was the first successful "talkie," a film that revolutionized the motion picture industry overnight.

New York's mayor during this breezy era was a dapper fellow named Jimmy Walker, elected by an adoring public in 1926 but dropped like a hot potato when graft, corruption, and assorted improprieties wiped the smile from his face. Mayor Jimmy was the candidate of the Tammany Hall Democratic machine; and when Governor Franklin D. Roosevelt appointed Samuel Seabury to investigate various departments of city government, Walker and other Tammany officials were put on the hot seat. Walker decided to resign suddenly before Governor Roosevelt had a chance to hear all the Seabury evidence. The investigation's revelations undoubtedly contributed to the rise of Fiorello H. La Guardia who, scorning the Tammany Tiger, ran on a Fusion ticket in 1933. Today, Jimmy Walker is remembered mainly as the author of that sentimental ballad, "Will You Love Me in December As You Did in May?" His handsome Anglo-Italian town house at 6 St. Luke's Place in the West Village is still standing.

Just as Gentleman Jimmy was bound to come crashing down after going up too far and too fast, the country, as it turned out, was destined to suffer the same fate. During the Roaring '20s—The Jazz Age—everyone, it seemed, was riding high . . . and so was the stock market. Butchers, bakers, candlestick makers, as well as magnates and movie stars, had a piece of the Wall Street action, and ticker tapes were read almost as much as the comics. Then the bust came—as it must when too few real assets are backing up too much paper.

Thursday, October 24, 1929—or Black Thursday, as it is recorded in financial history—was the day of mass selling, when investors in droves deserted the inflated market. The Wall Street morning started calmly enough, but panic had set in by 11:30 a.m.; and by the end of the day almost 13 million shares had changed hands. The disaster wiped out an estimated $30 million, at least on paper. As Historian Ellis observes:

> No one man was responsible for the crash. The get-rich-quick mania had afflicted almost everybody. About 9,000,000 savings accounts were wiped out, 85,000 businesses went to the wall, 5,000 banks failed, agriculture hit bottom, and national income was cut in half. New York and all America suffered the biggest jolt since the Civil War.

Thus began what economist John Kenneth Galbraith called "the most momentous economic occurrence in the history of the United States, the ordeal of the Great Depression."

FROM BREADLINES TO A WORLD'S FAIR

Unemployment was rampant. The apple sellers; the dispensers of pencils and shoelaces; the pathetic, hopeless souls with their tin cups sitting on street corners; the endless breadlines of proud but threadbare men patiently waiting at soup kitchens or parish-house doors for a daily ration of food for themselves and their starving families; the homeless sleeping everywhere, in parks, in the railroad stations, on subways, under bridges, even in cheap saloons, as well as missions and flophouses—the images of the Depression are burned into the fabric of the nation's social history. Arthur Miller, in his deeply felt play *The American Clock,* presents an unforgettable scene of two Midwestern farmers knocking on the door of a middle-class Jewish family in Brooklyn and looking for work. They are obviously starving, so the mother of the household serves them their first bowl of borscht, which they consume with relish though they have to ask what it is.

"Santas" are a frequent sight during the holidays.

According to accounts of the day, people actually did starve: four New York hospitals reported ninety-five such deaths in 1931. In 1932 alone, there were 1,595 suicides. In such an atmosphere, it is not surprising to learn that the American Communist Party thrived during the Depression years, organizing clubs throughout the New York City area and staging rallies and demonstrations (one of which turned into a massive riot on March 6, 1930) in Union Square, a popular spot for radical oratory.

An amusing (and revealing) story is told about Polly Adler, who for decades was the most famous "madam" in town, catering to some of the richest, most well-connected names. Polly was so intelligent and so witty that literary lights of the day like Robert Benchley used to drop by just to chat. After the Depression struck, Polly noticed a decided change in her clients' proclivities: they became far more interested in liquor than in sex. Forgetfulness was now a higher priority than physical stimulation.

Spectator sports offered another diversion for Depression-weary New Yorkers. Joe Louis became perhaps the greatest boxer of all time, winning the heavyweight championship in 1937, and in baseball Babe Ruth, Lou Gehrig, Joe DiMaggio, Carl Hubbell, and Mel Ott were Hall of Famers in the making.

Even though times were tough, the city, state, and nation were fortunate in their choice of political leaders. A New Yorker, Franklin Delano Roosevelt, was in the White House; Herbert H. Lehman, who was determined to run the racketeers out of New York, was in the governor's chair in Albany; and The Big Apple's own Fiorello ("Little Flower") H. La Guardia, born on Sullivan Street in Greenwich Village, was the new mayor. A Fusion candidate who pledged to clean up the mess left by Jimmy Walker, La Guardia was also a fusion person. He was short and stubborn, pudgy and pugilistic, lovable . . . and a liberal. His mother was Jewish, his father Italian-American, and he considered himself at one with all New Yorkers, no matter what their background. (When once accused—foolishly—of being anti-Semitic, he challenged his opponent to a debate . . . in Yiddish.) Totally honest and the consummate politician, he used his enormous influence and powers of persuasion to lead New York in a private and public building program that would take the sting out of the Depression. La Guardia Airport, the Brooklyn Battery Tunnel (linking Brooklyn and Manhattan), and the Lincoln Tunnel (linking midtown Manhattan with Weehawken, New Jersey) were engineering and construction marvels, and they all happened during La Guardia's twelve years (three terms) in office. Enormously popular, he had the common touch, and he was particularly fond of children. Once, during a newspaper strike, he read the funnies over the radio. Thomas Kessner, author of the definitive La Guardia biography, summed him up: "He made political integrity a civic habit, and by example he taught what dreams a committed honest leader could accomplish."

Aiding La Guardia in his ambitious programs for New York City was master builder Robert Moses (1888–1981) who learned early in life that the single most desirable prize the city can bestow is power. In his biography of Moses (1,246 pages of text and notes!), appropriately called *The Power Broker,* Robert A. Caro calls him "the single most powerful man of our time in the City and in the State of New York." A man of a many accomplishments (some of them extremely controversial) and multiple titles (Parks Commissioner was one), Moses rose to power during the '20s and held onto it for over forty years. Among his achievements are Jones Beach State Park, the Triborough Bridge, the

▲ St. Patrick's Cathedral in the snow—as it must have looked in the nineteenth century when sleighs, not limos, glided by its massive portal.

▶ St. Patrick's in summer.

▼ Cartier, one of Fifth Avenue's finest jewelry stores.

Verrazano-Narrows Bridge, the United Nations, Shea Stadium, Lincoln Center, the Cross Bronx Expressway, the 1964–65 World's Fair, and scores of parkways, playgrounds and swimming pools.

As already pointed out, magnificent new additions to the New York City skyline were planned and were well under way before the stock market crash—the Chrysler Building of 1930, and the Empire State Building, George Washington Bridge (connecting upper Manhattan and New Jersey), and new Waldorf-Astoria Hotel at Park Avenue and 50th Street, all 1931. Nevertheless, the boost they gave to a Depression-racked city cannot be denied. Thousands of workers were employed in their construction, and each new structure was a source of pride and a symbol of the prosperity that everyone believed was "just around the corner."

The Chrysler Building, the favorite skyscraper of many New Yorkers, held the title of the world's tallest building for only a few months before being outranked by the Empire State Building. Nevertheless, it is still the epitome of class. The gracefully scalloped, stainless steel Art Deco spire—brilliantly lighted at night with triangles of white neon tubing—is unique, as are the formidable-looking gargoyles (resembling the 1929 Chrysler

►► The Citicorp Center on Manhattan's East Side.

► St. Thomas Episcopal Church at Fifth Avenue and 53rd Street saw its first society wedding early in the century when Consuelo Vanderbilt married the Duke of Marlborough and has seen many more since. Its boys' choir and program of sacred music are justly famous.

▼ The sculpture garden at the Museum of Modern Art invites relaxation and contemplation amid the skyscrapers of midtown Manhattan.

hood ornaments that project from its fourth setback). The Art Moderne lobby—all African marble and chrome steel—is testimony to New York's unwritten architectural code: it is not enough to put up big buildings, they must also be works of art.

Although it is also no longer the world's (or even New York's) tallest building, the Empire State Building stands as proudly today as when it was formally opened on May 1, 1931. Another masterpiece of steel and limestone, the "great inland lighthouse" presides over midtown Manhattan—the quintessential skyscraper, daring any other building to give it competition. From the high-ceilinged, cathedral-like lobby, high-speed elevators whisk visitors to observation decks on the 86th and 102nd floors, from which more than 2 million visitors a year command the finest views of midtown Manhattan, Central Park, and upper New York City. Because the observatories are open every day until midnight, you have a chance to see the city dressed in its most romantic attire: a black velvet cape sprinkled with a million sparkling diamonds. Summer and the warm days of spring and fall are the most popular times at this 1,454-foot eagle's nest, but canny visitors, especially camera buffs, swear by the crystal-clear days of winter when you can see forever. People have jumped from the building (with and without parachutes), marathon runners dash up the stairs (86 floors of them!) in an annual competition, and notables from King Kong to Queen Elizabeth II have come to pay their respects. A star of the movies, the Empire State is usually cast as

► Four-story atrium in the Citicorp Center is a midtown oasis for shoppers and diners.

▼ The slant-top roof of the Citicorp Center was designed to catch the sun's rays, but this solar-heating project has yet to be put into operation.

This is the sight that greets travelers who come into Manhattan at night from the airports in Queens.

a *rendezvous d'amour*, as in *The Moon Is Blue* (a shocker in its day, 1953) and *On the Town* (with sailors Gene Kelly and Frank Sinatra jitterbugging with their gals, 1949). The building has been hit by lightning, hurricanes, migrating birds—even by a lost B-25 bomber during World War II—but it remains hale and hearty in advanced middle age, looking forward to celebrating the next holiday, when its spire will light up in green for St. Patrick's Day, purple for Easter, red, white, and blue for the Fourth of July, orange for Halloween, and red and green for the Christmas season.

Rockefeller Center, in the eyes of many the most beautiful and most notable urban development ever built, was constructed entirely within the Depression years and is therefore a symbol of the faith John D. Rockefeller, Jr., had in the future of his city. The initial group of buildings—fourteen in all—occupied 12 acres and included such landmarks as the seventy-story centerpiece RCA Building (now the GE Building, since 1989), the 6,000-seat Radio City Music Hall (world-famous for its precision dancers, the Rockettes, and annual "Christmas Spectacular" stage show), and the lovely Channel Gardens leading down to a sunken Lower Plaza, where visitors and residents alike flock for outdoor dining in summer and ice skating in winter. Grandly called "a city within a city," Rockefeller Center is nevertheless intensely human in concept with numerous parks and plazas, fountains and flowers

and dazzling pieces of Art Deco sculpture to please the senses and soften the massiveness of the project.

The very best way to experience Rockefeller Center, which has grown into a nineteen-building, 22-acre complex, is to take a self-guided tour (pick up a copy of the free folder, "Walking Tour of Rockefeller Center," in the lobby of the GE Building or at the Visitors Bureau, 2 Columbus Circle). Ever since the restoration of the spectacular Rainbow Room atop the GE Building and the redesign of its adjacent areas (like the Rainbow & Stars cabaret room), the observation roof has been closed, but you can still take guided tours of the NBC Studios and Radio City Music Hall, essential experiences for backstage buffs.

You could spend weeks touring Rockefeller Center and taking in its wonders, but even a short visit should include these stops: the gilded Prometheus statue fountain by Paul Manship in the Lower Plaza, John D. Rockefeller, Jr.'s "I Believe" credo at the entrance to the Lower Plaza, Lee Lawrie's heroic statue of Atlas in front of the International Building on Fifth Avenue, the Art Deco sculpture called "Wisdom" above the main entrance to the GE Building (30 Rockefeller Plaza), and the vast mural titled "American Progress" just inside across the back wall of the lobby. Downstairs, you will find a fascinating free exhibit on the history of the Center—plus hundreds of stores, boutiques, res-

121

taurants, and snack bars along miles of underground concourses. If you are fortunate to be in New York City at year-end holiday time—and the city is the most festive place to be during this joyous season—a visit to the Channel Gardens and the Lower Plaza is obligatory. A giant Christmas tree, brilliantly lighted, looms over the graceful form of Prometheus, and the gardens sparkle and shine with seasonal greenery and decorations. Excited children are everywhere and a thousand photographs are being taken every minute.

Two of the most important temples of New York's cultural life were added to the scene during the 1930s: the Hayden Planetarium and American Museum of Natural History (1935), and the original section of the Museum of Modern Art (1939), now greatly expanded by additions in the '50s, '60s, and '80s.

The Depression years were also a time of serious and diligent crime-fighting, and a young lawyer named Thomas E. Dewey turned out to be an even more persistent—and certainly more dramatic, as far as results were concerned—investigator than Samuel Seabury. On July 1, 1935, Dewey was appointed by New York County District Attorney William C. Dodge to act as a special assistant district attorney "to conduct an investigation of

vice and racketeering before an extraordinary grand jury." The new thirty-three-year-old special prosecutor moved quickly. By April 1936, he had jailed the crime boss of all bosses, "Lucky" Luciano, who was reported to control all the major rackets in Manhattan, Brooklyn, and Newark. Held without being able to raise the $350,000 bail (considered impossibly high at the time), Luciano was sentenced on July 18 to thirty to fifty years, along with other members of the gang. Dewey's sensational victory told the world he meant business, and it was followed by a string of other impressive convictions. Although the brilliant prosecutor went on to become governor, future political ambitions were thwarted when he ran up against master campaigner and man-of-the-people Harry Truman, who whistle-stopped himself to a popular victory over a good and honest man but one who came across as a stiff, rather chilly Easterner.

Just as disasters and tragedies often bring out the best in people, so the arts tend to flourish in periods of trial and tribulation. Hard times test the human spirit, and an examination of that spirit is what the arts are all about.

Many of the plays produced during the Depression fall into two categories. First: thoughtful, soulful plays that allowed audiences

▲ This tramway across the East River takes the residents of Roosevelt Island to and from work.

◄ The Queensboro Bridge, or 59th Street Bridge, which spans the East River, has appeared in countless films about New York.

to empathize with the struggles others were going through. Second: witty comedies (often with a social "message") and clever musicals that permitted theatergoers to escape the real world at least for a few hours.

On the serious side, Eugene O'Neill's retelling of the *Oresteia* by Aeschylus, *Mourning Becomes Electra* (1931), got the decade off to a distinguished and appropriately gloomy start. *Awake and Sing* by Clifford Odets in 1935 turned out to be one of the famous Group Theater's most successful productions, and its touching and humorous story of a lower-middle-class family in The Bronx brought some of the theater's most famous names to the stage: Luther Adler, Stella Adler, John Garfield, Morris Carnovsky, and Sanford Meisner. Maxwell Anderson's *Winterset* (a 1935 drama about the vengeful young son of an unjustifiably executed man) and *High Tor* (his 1937 play about the crooked schemes of an evil land grabber and a venal judge) were critical and popular successes, as was Sidney Kingsley's 1935 *Dead End*, with its famous East River waterfront set. Toward the end of the decade, two of the most acclaimed plays in American theater history were staged: Thornton Wilder's Pulitzer Prize winner *Our Town* (1938) and Lillian Hellman's *The Little Foxes* (1939), which gave stage legend Tallulah Bankhead her most famous role. Comedies of the era include the 1933 *Ah, Wilderness!* by Eugene O'Neill (a *lighthearted* look at his famous family), *Boy Meets Girl* (a 1935 Hollywood farce by Sam and Bella Spewack), Robert E. Sherwood's *Idiot's Delight* starring Alfred Lunt and Lynn Fontanne, and *You Can't Take It with You* by George S. Kaufman and Moss Hart (both 1936 and both Pulitzer Prize winners). Wrapping up the decade on a very high and funny note were *The Philadelphia Story,* written for Katharine Hepburn by Philip Barry, and *The Man Who Came To Dinner,* another Kaufman-Hart collaboration that gave Monty Woolley the plum role of Sheridan Whiteside.

(preceding pages) The bright lights of New York.

▼ A source of controversy with some critics, Philip Johnson's new AT&T Building at Madison Avenue and 56th Street *(top)* is nevertheless a hit with the public. And with its height and unique architecture, the building *(bottom)* easily holds its own in the Manhattan skyline.

► Dominating the lobby of the AT&T Building is the company's monumental symbol, "The Spirit of Communication," or "Golden Boy."

The 1930s were the first golden years of American musical comedy, and the hits came thick and fast. Musicals were nothing new to Broadway, of course, but before the '30s they generally fell into the revue, operetta or musical drama categories (*Ziegfeld Follies, The Desert Song, The Merry Widow,* and *Show Boat,* for example) rather than the witty, sophisticated shows that brightened the Depression years. Howard Dietz's *Three's a Crowd* (1930) starred Libby Holman, Fred MacMurray and Fred Allen and featured such song classics as "Body and Soul" and "Something to Remember You By." In 1931, Fred and Adele Astaire starred in *The Band Wagon* (a George S. Kaufman/ Howard Dietz/Arthur Schwartz production), and *Of Thee I Sing* (by Kaufman/Morris Ryskind/George and Ira Gershwin) introduced both "Who Cares?" and "Love Is Sweeping the Country" and won the first Pulitzer Prize for a musical. *Jubilee,* the Moss Hart-Cole Porter smash, at the decade's midpoint, contained such songs as "Begin the Beguine" and "Just One of Those Things," as well as the fledgling Montgomery Clift playing a young prince. The musically astonishing decade ended with two charmers: *The Boys from Syracuse* (1938), the Rodgers and Hart hit based on Shakespeare's *Comedy of Errors* and featuring such standards as "This Can't Be Love" and "Falling in Love with Love," and Cole Porter's *DuBarry Was a Lady* (1939), in which leather-lunged Ethel Merman belted out "Friendship" and "Katie Went to Haiti."

In other branches of the arts, dancer-choreographer Martha Graham exploded upon the scene in 1935, paving the way for such strictly American dancer/choreographers to come as Merce Cunningham, Paul Taylor, and Twyla Tharp. (One of the latest Graham ballets, *American Document,* premiered at the City Center in October 1989 when Miss Graham was 95!) Jazz, which

▲ An elegantly attired guard holds the door for visitors who come to gaze at the five-story atrium of the Trump Tower on Fifth Avenue.

(preceding pages) Georgia O'Keeffe, the noted American artist, painted dark and smoky skyline views much like this one when she lived in midtown Manhattan.

◄◄ Midtown Manhattan skyscrapers in close rank.

▼ Gleaming escalators at the Trump Tower whisk visitors up to the shops, boutiques, and cafés that line each floor.

The myriad setbacks on the Trump Tower façade bristle with Christmas trees each holiday season. At night their white lights add to the sparkle of the city.

▲ A giant, illuminated snowflake hangs over Fifth Avenue at 57th Street each Christmas.

▼ The grand auditorium of Carnegie Hall *(left)* has been noted for its fine acoustics ever since it opened in 1891. The Hall *(right)* was lovingly restored for its anniversary.

▲ A photograph of an eccentrically decorated tower on West 57th Street *(left)*. This imposing sculpture *(right)* marks the address of 9 West 57th Street.

► The old and the new coexist in midtown Manhattan. At right, the 1907 Plaza Hotel; at left, a ski-sloped modern skyscraper at 9 West 57th Street.

created a world sensation in the '20s, continued to flourish during the '30s, and New York was a magnet for all the stars. Duke Ellington, Count Basie, and Lena Horne appeared regularly at Harlem's Cotton Club, and the incomparable singer Billie Holiday (the musical daughter of Bessie Smith and Louis Armstrong) was at the peak of her genius in the late '30s, packing in her fans at Cafe Society, the Harlem jazz clubs and the joints along "Swing Street" (West 52nd). In 1938, jazz reached a Mt. Everest of sorts when Benny Goodman staged an astounding concert at Carnegie Hall with sidekicks Harry James, Gene Krupa, Lionel Hampton, Count Basie, and Teddy Wilson. George Gershwin, who demonstrated his affinity for blues and jazz in works like "Rhapsody in Blue" and "An American in Paris," proved his versatility with his magnificent opera *Porgy and Bess* in 1935. Modern movie fans are often surprised to learn that New York was a "Hollywood on the Hudson," so to speak, during the '30s. All of the earliest motion pictures made here naturally borrowed actors from the stage, and this trend continued during the Depression era, even though the entire motion picture industry eventually moved to California to take advantage of the more favorable year-round weather. Movies made locally were shot on the vast sound stages of the Kaufman-Astoria Studios in Queens,

The spacious plaza in front of the Plaza Hotel is filled with Christmas trees every year. The centerpiece Pulitzer Fountain, topped by a statue symbolizing abundance, is where Zelda Fitzgerald took some highly publicized midnight dips.

and most of the actors were appearing on Broadway at the same time during the evenings. Jack Benny, Clara Bow, Burns and Allen, Maurice Chevalier, Claudette Colbert, Gary Cooper, W. C. Fields, Danny Kaye, Laurence Olivier, Ginger Rogers, Gloria Swanson, and Rudolph Valentino are among the stars who crossed the East River to face the cameras. The Marx Brothers made their first two films, *The Cocoanuts* and *Animal Crackers,* in the Astoria Studios; Paul Robeson made the film version of Eugene O'Neill's *The Emperor Jones* and Nöel Coward starred in *The Scoundrel.* Today, the studios are once again making movies— plus all of the episodes of TV's top-rated *Cosby Show.* Next to the Studios, the American Museum of the Moving Image opened in 1988, the nation's only facility celebrating the art, history, and technology of film and television. The AMMI collection consists of 60,000 artifacts: scenery, costumes, props, annotated scripts, publicity photographs, posters, production set models, lobby cards, souvenirs, fan magazines, and historical and state-of-the-art technical equipment. You can stroll through a movie set, watch excerpts from classics on TV screens, see full-length films in a 190-seat theater, picture yourself—via a "magic mirror"—as Vivien Leigh in *Gone With the Wind* or Sylvester Stallone in *Rocky,* and add to your own cinema collection in the museum shop.

Even movies made in Hollywood during the 1930s had a fascination for New York City stories and locales. In addition to the already mentioned *King Kong,* films set in New York included *42nd Street, The Great Ziegfeld, Dead End, Nothing Sacred, Stage Door, You Can't Take It With You, Dark Victory, The Women,* and *My Man Godfrey,* wherein Carole Lombard, playing a rich girl on a scavenger hunt, finds a victim of the Depression— a "forgotten man"—in a huge garbage dump in the borough of Queens . . . the same dump that became the setting for the 1939–40 World's Fair.

As if to blow away the Depression decade with a blast of optimism, the city fathers decided to celebrate the 150th anniversary of George Washington's first oath of office with a gigantic preview of "The World of Tomorrow." And so New York's first World's Fair—with its symbols, the Perisphere and Trilon—rose on the "Corona Dump" (now Flushing Meadows-Corona Park), the eerie, ashy wasteland described so vividly by F. Scott Fitzgerald in *The Great Gatsby.*

▲ A sidewalk painter.

▼ Plaza Hotel guests *(left)* learn that taxis can be scarce during snowstorms. Richly decorated inside and out, the Plaza *(right)* has been restored to its white-and-gold splendor.

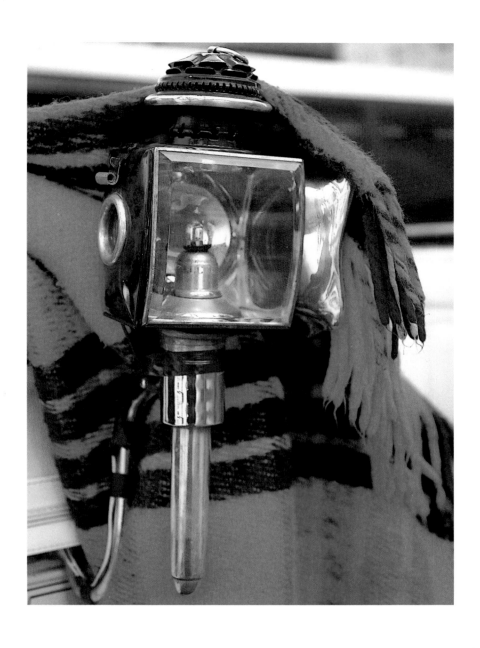

◄▲ A lamp and a lap robe decorate a horse-drawn carriage. Visitors and residents love the old-time splendor of the city's horse-drawn carriages.

▼ Portable bookstalls on Central Park South are a favorite with browsers.

▲ Some of New York City's policemen at the edge of Central Park.

▶ ▶ Mounted patrolmen are particularly effective in controlling crowds.

WORLD WAR II TO WORLD'S FAIR II

Just when New Yorkers were beginning to believe there really was a bright new "World of Tomorrow," along came December 7, 1941, and everyone dug in for another duration. In many ways, New York City was an exciting place to be during World War II. Masses of people always coming and going . . . troops either on their way to the war zones or coming home . . . servicemen, unable to find room at the inn, sleeping in hotel lobbies . . . businessmen going about the business of war . . . women, taking over the war-plant jobs, wrapping bandages for the Red Cross, and helping to boost morale by hostessing at the USO and the Stage Door Canteen . . . patriotic citizens joining the Civil Air Patrol and volunteering as air raid wardens, patrolling the streets and making sure the blackout regulations were strictly observed . . . everyone saving their cooking fats and tin cans and buying War Stamps and pasting them in their War Bond booklets.

So great was the strain on La Guardia Airport that the mayor broke ground for Idlewild Airport in Queens in 1941, a facility that has grown into today's massive JFK complex. The mayor's duties and responsibilities were growing as fast as the city and the war effort, and it was decided that he needed a proper mayor's

mansion instead of being forced to pick and pay for his own lodgings. Gracie Mansion, a lovely 1799 Federal-style wooden country house overlooking the East River at 88th Street, was selected and refurbished, and Mayor La Guardia and his family became the first official occupants in 1942. (Since then numerous improvements and restorations have taken place and an addition for entertaining was built in 1966.)

Perhaps New York's greatest contribution to the war effort was the Federal contract to Columbia University scientists in 1940 to carry out super-secret research on a program that became known as the Manhattan Project. Its objective was to develop the first atomic bomb. (The uranium atom had already been split in Columbia's cyclotron laboratory at Broadway and 120th Street on January 25, 1939.) Although New York was never as notorious a spy center as, say, Lisbon or Vienna, sneaky things did happen here during the war years. The French liner *Normandie,* which had been converted to a troop ship, mysteriously caught fire and sank at its pier on the Hudson River. (A glimpse of the huge vessel on its side may be seen in Alfred Hitchcock's 1942 film, *Saboteur,* during a chase that starts in Radio City Music Hall and ends up atop the Statue of Liberty.)

▲ Central Park, an 840-acre green carpet in midtown Manhattan, is actually larger than Monaco!

◄ Looking west, over Central Park, during a fine day in midtown Manhattan.

In those days before television, New Yorkers sought diversion on Broadway and at the movies. The big hit plays on the boards included Shirley Booth in *My Sister Eileen,* Helen Hayes and Maurice Evans in *Twelfth Night,* Ethel Barrymore in *The Corn Is Green,* Paul Muni in *Counsellor-at-Law* and Margaret Sullavan in *The Voice of the Turtle,* a wartime love story about a New York gal who lets a GI guy spend his leave in her apartment during the housing crisis. Musicals of the period included Ethel Waters in *Cabin in the Sky,* Gene Kelly in *Pal Joey,* the phenomenal *Oklahoma!* (the first Richard Rodgers and Oscar Hammerstein II collaboration), and *Carmen Jones,* a modern version of Bizet's *Carmen* with an all-Black cast headed by Muriel Smith (and in the later film version by Dorothy Dandridge, Harry Belafonte, and Pearl Bailey). Movies of the day tended to be frothy entertainments like Lucille Ball's *Best Foot Forward* or the June Allyson-Gloria DeHaven-Van Johnson romp, *Two Girls and a Sailor,* morale boosters like *The Pride of the Yankees* (Gary Cooper as Lou Gehrig) or *Yankee Doodle Dandy* (James Cagney in his Oscar-winning performance as George M. Cohan), or New York-based mysteries like *The House on 92nd Street* (a spy thriller) and *Laura,* with the hauntingly beautiful Gene Tierney. But there were "serious" films, too: for example, Ray Milland as the alcoholic in *The Lost Weekend* and James Dunn, faced with the same trouble, in *A Tree Grows in Brooklyn*—both of whom copped an Academy Award for their performances.

Finally, after a four-year struggle, the war was over—on August 14, 1945—and a mass celebration broke out spontaneously in Times Square and throughout the city. Everyone had reason to

▲ Wollman Skating Rink draws fresh-air fans during the crisp, clear days of winter.

◄ The Plaza Hotel and other midtown Manhattan buildings are reflected in the southeast pond of Central Park.

(following pages) Bicycling is a popular Central Park sport, especially on days when the park roads are closed to automobile traffic.

be joyous, but many also had reason to be bitter: out of some 900,000 New Yorkers in uniform, over 16,000 were killed, wounded, or reported missing in action.

New Yorkers who lived through them generally consider the twenty years following World War II to be a golden time, "the best years to be in New York," you'll hear them say. Actually, when you consider that the years 1945–65 followed a world-wide disaster, they were pretty good times anywhere, by comparison. U.S. citizens everywhere were anxious to settle down, to "get back to normal" and resume building that bright future the World's Fair told them would be theirs. Veterans went back to school in droves on the GI Bill, and local universities such as Columbia and New York University were bursting their seams.

Building projects, long delayed by the war, were given the green light, and the next two decades produced some of the city's most notable architectural landmarks—many of them on Park Avenue, which was *the* avenue to be on. (New Yorkers then tended to cluster in fashionable areas; it was not until more recent years that high rents and space shortages forced them to disperse.) Lever House, that beautiful green slab at Park Avenue and 53rd Street, was the first of the postwar avant-garde, metal-and-glass

curtain-wall skyscrapers in 1952, and it was followed by the stunning 1958 Seagram Building (the work of Mies van der Rohe, with Philip Johnson designing the ground-floor Four Seasons restaurant), the 1960 Union Carbide Building, and the 1963 Pan Am Building, which looms over Park Avenue and Grand Central Terminal.

The United Nations is by far the period's most ambitious project in both scope and political significance. Looking today at this dazzling, 18-acre complex of buildings, gardens, plazas, promenades and hundreds of art works (both inside and out) spread out along the East River from 42nd to 48th streets, it is difficult to believe that this area once teemed with abatoires, breweries, and slum housing. The magician who effected the startling change was John D. Rockefeller, Jr., who purchased the land and presented the site to the U.N. as the location of its permanent headquarters. President Harry S. Truman laid the cornerstone of the project in 1949 and the first General Assembly session was held in 1952. An international team of architects, headed by Wallace K. Harrison (of Rockefeller Center fame), designed a group of buildings that, according to most critical and popular opinions, is both attractive and functional.

143

The two most prominent buildings are the tall and narrow (544 feet high by 72 feet thick) Secretariat Building and the low and slab-like General Assembly Building.

Today, the United Nations is high on the list of any visitor's "must" list. Even the U.N.'s severest critics admit that the complex is an impressive sight and that the forums held there are at least a safety valve for world tensions and a platform where world problems can be aired if not solved. One could spend days attending U.N. meetings (tickets are free, on a first-come, first-served basis, at the Information Desk in the General Assembly lobby), but at least a half-day should be spent taking a guided tour, strolling through the peaceful, well-kept gardens, admiring the unusual works of art that are gifts from all over the world (one of the latest is a 1988 sculpture from Luxembourg: a giant pistol with its barrel tied in a knot), and browsing the shops in the General Assembly's basement (including an international bazaar, a book shop, and the U.N.'s own post office with stamps that can be used only there). The spacious Delegates Dining Room is open to the public on most days by reservation, and there is a very inexpensive coffee shop near the basement gift shop. Because this is U.N. territory, no tax is levied anywhere in the complex.

Any sports fan will tell you that the darkest time on the postwar horizon was the year the beloved Brooklyn Dodgers left town (1956), a year in which the equally beloved Ebbets Field was turned into a housing project.

▶ A street musician entertains passersby.

▼ Cherry trees and daffodils in exuberant bloom.

▲ If Central Park's fresh air stimulates the appetite, a hot dog is always close at hand.

▼ The New York Marathon kicks off each fall, starting in Staten Island and ending in Central Park, after touching all five boroughs of the city.

On the cultural front, the city's most important acquisition in the postwar years was the Guggenheim Museum, Frank Lloyd Wright's only public structure in New York, which was completed in 1959 across from Central Park at Fifth Avenue and 89th Street. Controversial from the start (as were almost all of Wright's works), the building has been called everything from a giant snail to a large toilet bowl. Over the years it has proved to be great fun and a most enjoyable space for viewing pictures and sculptures. Because you take an elevator to the top of the building and stroll down a spiral ramp, there is no chance of getting lost (as often happens in the Chinese-box layouts of many museums). One side of the ramp is open to a central atrium, the other side—the wall side—is where the works of art are displayed. Modern masters such as Kandinsky, Chagall, Léger, Cézanne, Miró, Klee, Picasso, Braque, Pollock, Mondrian, de Kooning, Brancusi, Calder, and Henry Moore are the strengths of the collection, and there is also a separate collection—the Thannhauser bequest, displayed by itself in a special wing—that is especially rich in Impressionist and Neo-Impressionist paintings: Manet, Matisse, Picasso, Renoir, Cézanne, Van Gogh, Gauguin, Degas, and Toulouse-Lautrec.

If one of the theater's primary functions is to entertain, Broadway played its role superbly in the two postwar decades. Cheering up a war-weary town and its millions of visitors were some of the finest musicals in the history of The Great White Way: Cole Porter's greatest musical *Kiss Me Kate* (1948); Mary Martin (washing that man right out of her hair) and Ezio Pinza in Rodgers and Hammerstein's *South Pacific* (1949); Frank Loesser's *Guys and Dolls* (1950); Ethel Merman playing the U.S. ambassador to Luxembourg in *Call Me Madam* (1950); Yul Brynner's regal *The King and I* (1951); *Kismet,* which turned the music of Borodin into a Main Stem operetta; Rosalind Russell in Leonard Bernstein's

▲ February snow *(top)* can turn Central Park's Mall into a winter wonderland, while tulips *(bottom)* herald the arrival of spring.

▶ An artist at work under the cherry blossoms in Central Park.

▲ Familiarly known as "the boat pond," Central Park's Conservatory Waters *(left)* draws interested spectators of all ages. The miniature boats sailed on the Conservatory Waters *(right)* often show exquisite workmanship and detail, like this handsome schooner.

►► Elegant Fifth Avenue high-rises overlook Central Park.

▼ A statue of Alice in Wonderland can be found at the north end of the boat pond.

◀ Top to bottom:

Winding lanes, picturesque bridges, flowers, and blossoming shrubs make Central Park a stroller's paradise.

Entertainers perform in the plaza of the Bethesda Fountain.

"The Angel of the Waters," crowning the lovely Bethesda Fountain in Central Park, was sculpted by Emma Stebbins in 1868.

▼ The pinnacled gables of The Dakota rise above Central Park Lake.

▲ Rent a rowboat, head for the middle of the lake, and you could be miles from the traffic's roar.

► Top to bottom:

Sunlight illumines graceful details of the elegant, cast-iron Bow Bridge designed by Calvert Vaux in 1879.

Bow Bridge spans the lake and leads to a wild and bosky section called the Ramble.

The apartment towers of Central Park West, with The Dakota in the foreground.

(preceding pages) The skyline of Central Park West.

◄ Top to bottom:

People ski in the park when the snow arrives!

John Lennon's widow, Yoko Ono, gave the city this "Imagine" memorial in the "Strawberry Fields" section of the Park.

Belvedere Castle tops an eminence overlooking the Delacorte Theater, where free Shakespeare plays are presented each summer.

► Sunset turns the buildings of upper Fifth Avenue to red and gold. At right is Frank Lloyd Wright's extraordinary Guggenheim Museum, his only public building in New York City.

Wonderful Town (1953); *Damn Yankees,* Gwen Verdon's homerun hit (1955); *My Fair Lady,* perhaps the wittiest, most sophisticated musical ever, with Rex Harrison as Professor Henry Higgins and Julie Andrews as Eliza Doolittle (1956); two Leonard Bernstein musicals that broke new ground in both style and content—*Candide* (1956) and *West Side Story* (1957); *The Music Man,* wherein Robert Preston turned River City upside down (1957); *Gypsy,* which gave Ethel Merman, composer Jule Styne and lyricist Stephen Sondheim one of their finest hours (1959); *The Sound of Music,* another megahit from Rodgers and Hammerstein starring Mary Martin (1959); *How to Succeed in Business Without Really Trying,* which had a run as long as its title (1961); another long-title, long-run show, *A Funny thing Happened on the Way to the Forum* (1962); two top shows for two top ladies, both in 1963—Barbra Streisand's *Funny Girl* and Carol Channing's *Hello, Dolly!; Fiddler on the Roof,* the "sleeper" hit that ran forever (1964); and Angela Lansbury's lovable *Mame* (1965).

The 1945–65 period was also a rich one for comedies and dramas. The golden immortals include Tennessee Williams' *A Streetcar Named Desire* (1947); Arthur Miller's *Death of a Salesman* (1949); Carson McCullers' *Member of the Wedding* (1950); Tennessee Williams's *Cat on a Hot Tin Roof* (1955); Kim Stanley creating the role of Cherie in *Bus Stop* (1955); Paul Muni in *Inherit the Wind* (1955); *The Diary of Anne Frank* (1955); Eugene O'Neill's greatest play—and one many consider the finest by an American writer—*Long Day's Journey Into Night* (1956); Tennessee Williams's *Sweet Bird of Youth* with Geraldine Page and Paul Newman (1959); Lorraine Hansberry's *A Raisin in the Sun* (1959); Tennessee Williams's last big hit, *The Night of the Iguana* (1961); Edward Albee's most famous work, *Who's Afraid of Virginia Woolf?* (1962); and Neil Simon's *The Odd Couple* (1964).

In Hollywood's eyes, postwar New York proved as photogenic as ever, and more and more of the films were being shot on location and less and less in the studio. Among them were: *The Jolson Story* and *Miracle on 34th Street,* wherein the real star was the Macy's Thanksgiving Day Parade (both 1946); *Gentleman's Agreement,* which tackled the ticklish subject of bigotry (1947); *Adam's Rib,* with Hepburn and Tracy, and *The Heiress,* with Olivia de Havilland as Henry James's heroine (1949); *All About Eve,* which gave Bette Davis and the New York theater their greatest roles, and Judy Holliday in *Born Yesterday* (both in 1950); Marlon Brando in *On the Waterfront* (1954); Ernest Borgnine in *Marty* (1955); Elizabeth Taylor in *Butterfield 8* and Shirley MacLaine and Jack Lemmon in *The Apartment,* two

cynical views of professional guys and gals in Manhattan (1960); and the all-stops-out movie version of *West Side Story* (1961).

The twenty-year period following the war ended on two appropriately upbeat notes. The Verrazano-Narrows Bridge, connecting Brooklyn with Staten Island, opened on November 21, 1964; it spanned the entrance to New York harbor and gave the city the world's largest suspension bridge. (The main span is 4,260 feet long, 60 feet longer than the Golden Gate Bridge in San Francisco.) And the opening of the 1964–65 World's Fair—on the same Flushing Meadows site as the 1939–40 fair—gave New Yorkers and more than 10 million visitors a chance to wonder at current and future technology, to marvel at some of the greatest art the world has ever produced, to tour the world in scores of foreign pavilions, and to savor the specialties of a dozen different ethnic cuisines. The Disney exhibits and rides were the kids' favorites; the Danish and Spanish restaurants were the top reservations in town (followed by the Pavilion of Gas restaurant, which was everyone's favorite World's Fair name); and Michaelangelo's "Pietà" (sent by the Vatican) and Goya's "The Naked Maja" (lent by the Prado) were the most popular

► Cleopatra's Needle, an ancient Egyptian obelisk standing near the Metropolitan Museum of Art in Central Park, is the twin of one standing on the Victoria Embankment in London.

►► The Metropolitan Museum of Art (1879) can be found along Fifth Avenue between 80th and 84th Streets.

▼ In the old days, the path along the Central Park Reservoir was where athletes, especially boxers, did their roadwork. Now, any New Yorker eager to keep fit enjoys running there.

▲ The Metropolitan is so rich in art treasures that only a portion of them can be exhibited at any one time.

▼ Behind the glass façade is the Temple of Dendur, a gift of the Egyptian Government to the Metropolitan Museum of Art.

art works. An ironic fact about the fair is that it drew more New Yorkers and fewer out-of-towners than expected. The explanation is that the fair had to compete with the great attractions of New York that were already in place, and consequently visitors found they couldn't tear themselves away from the city's theaters, museums, sightseeing attractions, restaurants, sports events, music and dance performances, shops, and stores long enough to take the subway ride out to Willets Point in Queens.

THE BIG APPLE BECOMES THE WORLD'S CAPITAL

The two and one-half decades following the second World's Fair were times of trouble and triumph, crises and celebrations as the city rode a roller coaster between its highs and lows.

The Big Blackout of 1965—a sudden and massive power outage—plunged the entire city into total darkness just as the work day was ending, but everyone behaved beautifully, neighbor helping neighbor through the long night. (During the second big blackout in 1977, looting was reported in some neighborhoods, but the city soon regained its poise.)

The next few years did not go smoothly in The Big Apple. Riots broke out in the East New York section of Brooklyn and in the East Harlem section of upper Manhattan in 1966–67, while

◀ The Great Hall of the Metropolitan on a quiet day. When the museum hosts a special exhibition, there is hardly standing room in this area.

▼ One of the museum's treasures, ''Perseus with the Head of Medusa.''

Columbia University students staged campus-wide protests and riots in 1968. Throughout the city at this time, especially in the vicinity of the U.N., protests against the war in Vietnam were regular occurrences.

The early 1970s found New York at its lowest ebb, plagued with fiscal crisis and facing bankruptcy. Anti-New York feeling was at an all-time high, with Johnny Carson nightly poking fun at the town's troubles and President Gerald Ford's attitude summed up in a famous *New York Daily News* headline, FORD TO CITY: DROP DEAD. Most Americans felt the same way—let it sink, they said—until they realized that as New York goes, so goes the nation. Ultimately, the fiscal crisis was a lesson in united-we-stand, divided-we-fall political science.

The financial bailout—a joint effort on the Federal, state and local levels, with a big assist from economic experts in private industry—was the beginning of another period of ascendency for New York.

As the size and prestige of New York City has grown over the years, the office of its mayor has increased in importance to the point where it is described as the second-most-difficult political office in the nation. (Many even consider it the most difficult

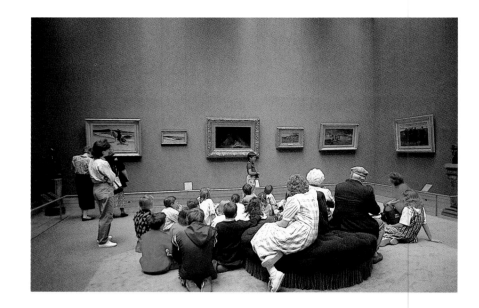

▲ Paintings and other *objets d'art* are placed for easy contemplation.

▼ ► Two views of the Temple of Dendur. Because the structure is enclosed within an all-glass building, the stones "change colors" throughout the day, adding a further dimension of interest for the visitor.

▲ On display in the glass-enclosed garden of the American Wing are examples of sculpture and statuary, mostly from the nineteenth century.

◄ This marble façade—all that remains of an 1826 Greek Revival building that once was the New York branch of the Bank of the United States—adds a note of grandeur to the garden.

post because New York's mayor does not have the resources and personnel at his disposal that the president has.) In the last four decades, there have been six mayors, and each has put his distinctive stamp on city affairs as well as on city politics. In fact, the power of New York's mayor is a measurable force in the city's social, business, and cultural life, and in many ways his personality and personal style determine the mood of the city. William O'Dwyer (elected 1946) had extensive experience in civic life, but his time in office was plagued with troubles and tainted with scandal and he was forced to resign; Vincent R. Impellitteri, City Council President, filled out his second term. Robert F. Wagner, Jr. (1953) was calm, intelligent and patient—an effective negotiator and the consummate politician. John V. Lindsay (1965), the Republican who turned Democrat, was handsome, stylish, and intellectual—a class act who improved the image of the city during difficult times in spite of the kidding he took about calling New York "Fun City." Abraham D. Beame (1974) was a capable man—a devoted Big Apple fan and extremely well versed in financial affairs (he had served as Comptroller)—but fiscal woes dogged his term and he was blamed (unfairly) for the city's plight. Edward I. Koch (1978), New York's most famous mayor since La Guardia (his idol) was a dyed-in-the-wool New Yorker—volatile, sharp in his opinions, frank to a fault. An astute—even brilliant—politician, he made an exciting, colorful, highly

◄ The eccentric, but highly praised, architecture of the Whitney Museum complements one of the finest collections of American art in the world.

▼ The Fifth Avenue home of millionaire Henry Clay Frick *(top)*, with his incomparable collection of fine art, is now an exquisite small museum open to the public. The garden of the Frick Museum *(bottom)*.

▲ Critics have likened Frank Lloyd Wright's Guggenheim Museum to everything from the Queen Mum's hat to a corkscrew.

► Paintings and sculptures at the Guggenheim Museum are arranged around a central ramp that spirals down from a dazzling skylight.

(following pages) The Cloisters in upper Manhattan's Fort Tryon Park is a branch of the Metropolitan Museum of Art devoted solely to medieval art and architecture.

visible mayor, and he was always good for a quote; but the scandals that rocked his administration and his inability to soothe tensions finally brought Mr. Big Apple down.

Perhaps this is the proper place to point out exactly *how* New York City became known as The Big Apple. Although the term sounds new, it had actually been used back in the 1920s and '30s by Harlem jazz musicians and by entertainment and sports figures as a way of saying, "I'm playing New York City—I've made it to the big time!" Or, when jazz bands played their gigs in one-night stands, hopping from place to place, they used to say, "There are many apples on the tree, but when you pick New York, you pick *the big apple!*" Among the outgrowths of the saying was a dance called The Big Apple and a famous Harlem bar bearing that name. Nevertheless, the term remained an esoteric one, known only to a certain segment of the cultural scene, until the New York Convention & Visitors Bureau selected it in 1971 as the theme of its entire marketing and promotion campaign. At the time, the perception across the world was that everything bad happened in New York. This was ridiculous, of course, but because the news media are centered in the city, an inordinate

▲ A stroll among the treasures of The Cloisters transports visitors to another day.

▼ Beautifully carved capitals from European medieval structures have found a home at The Cloisters.

amount of space was given to crime (when, in reality, New York has never been number one in crime statistics—or even close to the top—as an examination of FBI statistics will prove).

The purpose of The Big Apple campaign was not to deny the city's problems—problems all urban centers share these days—but to put matters into fair and reasonable perspective. The objective was to emphasize the city's positive advantages and to remind visitors what an exciting and enriching experience awaited them in . . .The Big Apple. The program was an enormous success; the media and the general public stopped selling New York short, and both visitors and conventions began to increase steadily. Today, tourism is second only to garment-fashion as the city's fastest-growing industry, bringing in some 20 million visitors and $10 billion each year.

With its fortunes and spirits on the rise, The Big Apple embarked on another building boom, one that continues unabated to this day. The new (and fourth) Madison Square Garden, which had opened in 1968, proved to be a great success, not only as a splendid sports palace but as an arena for such outstanding events as the annual visit of the circus and the Democratic National Conventions of 1976 and 1980. The World Trade Center, which opened in sections as buildings were completed during the early 1970s, was the keystone project that led to the boom lower Manhattan is now enjoying. The Center's outdoor observation deck (the world's highest) on the roof above Tower 1 is thronged with visitors every good-weather day (in August 1989 it welcomed its 20 millionth visitor!); Windows on the World, the dazzling restaurant atop Tower 1, is as notable for its cuisine as it is for its views; and the Vista International, the only hotel in the area, has been a smash hit.

On the landfill for the vast World Trade Center complex has risen another city within the city—called Battery Park City. An

▲ The hilltop setting of The Cloisters, overlooking the broad Hudson River, is as spectacular as the medieval art treasures it contains.

▼ Le Corbusier called the George Washington Bridge in upper Manhattan "the most beautiful bridge in the world."

▲ President Ulysses S. Grant, after a stormy army career and a presidency burdened with troubles, was laid to rest in this tomb on Manhattan's Upper West Side. His wife, Julia, is also buried here.

► The impressive dome of Grant's Tomb, officially known as General Grant National Memorial.

►► The carillon of Riverside Church fills the Upper West Side with music, and the views from the church tower are spectacular.

enormous development on 92 acres, it stretches from Battery Park to Chambers Street along the Hudson River, and it contains the shining towers (obviously related but each a different size and shape to please the eye) of the World Financial Center, which contains the headquarters of such firms as American Express, Merrill Lynch, and Dow Jones. As amenities, there are smart shops and stores on two levels, a soaring crystal-palace Winter Garden planted with sixteen palm trees, a Courtyard with several fine (and inexpensive) restaurants, an enormous plaza overlooking river and harbor, and a North Cove boat basin where sleek yachts from all over the world tie up. South of the World Financial Center, along the Hudson, is a gracious, tree-lined esplanade, interspersed with gardens, outdoor sculptures, and neighbor-hoods built around new apartment houses. It is a perfect place to spend a Sunday in New York.

Other exciting additions to the city's skyline include the 1977 Citicorp Center, the silver, slant-roofed tower at 53rd Street between Third and Lexington avenues; the 1987 IBM building, with its enclosed bamboo garden and its free IBM Gallery of Science and Art, at 57th Street and Madison Avenue; the 1983 Trump Tower, one of the town's most popular tourist attractions, at Fifth Avenue and 56th Street, with five stories of boutiques,

▲ Work on the vast Cathedral of St. John the Divine at Amsterdam Avenue and West 112th Street *(left and right)*, begun in 1892, is moving toward completion. Stones for St. John the Divine are being cut by master masons following the same methods used by the craftsmen who built Europe's great cathedrals.

► A memorial to the Civil War dead, the Soldiers' and Sailors' Monument is a familiar landmark of Riverside Park on the Upper West Side.

restaurants, and cafés surrounding a soaring central atrium and its 80-foot waterfall; the 1984 AT&T Building (Philip Johnson's Chippendale-style tower a block down from IBM, containing a high, cross-vaulted lobby holding Evelyn Longworth's famous statue, "The Spirit of Communication," or "Golden Boy," as it is popularly known); the 1986 Equitable Center (a fifty-three-story skyscraper with Roy Lichtenstein's huge—68 feet by 32 feet—mural in its 80-foot arched entranceway, which also contains a branch of the Whitney Museum); and the 1986 Jacob K. Javits Convention Center (I. M. Pei's monumental steel and glass crystal palace overlooking the Hudson River at West 34th Street).

Incidentally, the atrium concept in the city's newer buildings—or the idea of devoting open space to public use—was pioneered by Rockefeller Center with its parks and plazas. Other trend-setting structures are the 1958 Seagram Building on Park Avenue and the 1967 Ford Foundation Building near the U.N. on East 42nd Street. The latter's jungle-like interior garden, with its trees and plants surrounding a forest pool, is a wonder to behold.

The 1970s and '80s were also times of joyous celebrations in New York City. Although Philadelphia was the epicenter of

Erected in 1902, the marble monument of the Soldiers' and Sailors' Monument is modeled on the Choragic Monument of Lysicrates in Athens.

the July 4, 1976, celebrations of the nation's Declaration of Independence, the largest and most colorful festivities were held in New York and its magnificent harbor. Tall sailing ships—in a regatta called "Operation Sail"—came from all over the world to salute the U.S.A. on its 200th birthday, and they were joined by thousands of naval and civilian craft. Topping off the four-day celebration were massive fireworks displays bursting above the harbor and the Statue of Liberty.

Ticker-tape parades are a New York invention. The tapes of the old Wall Street days have now been replaced by confetti, computer print-outs and shredded office documents. There have been three memorable parades in recent years; in 1969 when the Apollo 11 crew (Neil Armstrong, Edwin E. Aldrin, Jr., and Michael Collins) came back from their moonwalks, in 1986 when the Amazin' Mets became the kings of baseball, and in 1981 when New York saluted the fifty-two American hostages held captive by Iran for 444 days.

The Brooklyn Bridge's centennial celebration in 1983, though not as large or as international in scope as the birthday bashes for the nation and Statue of Liberty, was nevertheless one of New York City's finest hours. So majestic is "The Great Bridge"—and so beloved by all New Yorkers—that its 100th anniversary was of major historic and social importance to New Yorkers who walk or drive across it on the way to and from work, sail under it on excursions, or simply admire it from a hundred different vantage points. There were books written about it and documentaries filmed; magazines scheduled cover stories; and TV news programs and talk shows were alive with bridge updates and reminiscences.

The fireworks that lighted the bridge on its birthday were truly spectacular.

The 200th anniversary of George Washington's first inauguration, held at Federal Hall in New York City on April 30, 1789, was another event of national, even international, importance. Once again, the world was reminded that New York was the nation's first capital (from September 13, 1788 to December 6, 1790); that the first U.S. Congress convened here (March 6, 1789); and the U.S. Supreme Court was established here (September 24, 1789).

Because Washington's oath of office was administered on the balcony of Federal Hall, at the junction of Wall and Broad streets, that spot was selected as the focus of the bicentennial celebrations. The historic ceremony was recreated, President George Bush delivered a patriotic address, the descendents of past presidents were in attendance, choirs sang, politicians waved, the threatening rain held off, and a thousand balloons and masses of confetti clouded the skies. During the long weekend, services were conducted at St. Paul's Chapel (where Washington worshipped after his inaugural address), a symposium on the presidency in the 1990s was held at Fordham University, a Grand Parade ("Bicentennial Procession") marched from Federal Hall to City Hall; a Parade of Ships (or "Presidential Flotilla") took place in the harbor, and the inevitable fireworks spectacular exploded in the skies over the East River at the foot of Wall Street.

Modern American art came into its own following World War II, and in the last four decades the works of such New York-based artists as Andy Warhol, Jasper Johns, Roy Lichtenstein,

▲ New York's largest museum, the American Museum of Natural History, faces Central Park between 77th and 81st streets.

Louise Nevelson, Willem de Kooning, Isamu Noguchi, Robert Rauschenberg, Larry Rivers, Richard Serra, and Helen Frankenthaler attracted worldwide attention—and astronomical prices. To hold their works, the Museum of Modern Art doubled its size, the Whitney Museum opened branches all over town, and the Metropolitan opened a separate wing devoted to modern art. Although many consider New York a constant, never-ending festival of the arts, the city-wide First New York International Festival of the Arts was held in the summer of 1988, and its success guaranteed its periodic return.

Chronic grumblings from the critics about the state of theater in New York are an accepted fact of cultural life in The Big Apple. Nevertheless, the last two decades have added luster to theater history and prompted enthusiastic response from audiences. Stephen Sondheim has emerged as the modern master of musicals with such credits as *Company* (1970), *Follies* (1971), *A Little Night Music* (1972), *Pacific Overtures* (1975), *Sweeney Todd* (1979), *Sunday in the Park With George* (1983, a Pulitzer-Prize winner), and *Into the Woods* (1987). The late Michael Bennett had a brief but incandescent career, and his masterpiece, *A Chorus Line* (1975), revolutionized the American musical, cutting out patterns that others will copy for years to come. Other hit musicals of the past twenty years included *Cabaret* (1966), *Hair* (the 1968 "hippie" musical that has steadily grown in stature since creating its initial shock waves), *Grease* (1971, one of the longest runs in theater history), *The Wiz* (1974, which began weakly and ended up a smash), *For Colored Girls . . .* (1976), *Annie* (the 1976 blockbuster), *Sugar Babies* (1979, the perfect vehicle for old troupers Ann Miller and Mickey Rooney), *42nd Street* (the 1980 hit whose director/

choreographer Gower Champion died on opening night), *Sophisticated Ladies* (1980), *Ain't Misbehavin'* (which resurrected Fats Waller and made Nell Carter a star, 1981), *Nine* (1981), *La Cage aux Folles* (1983), *Big River* (1984), *The Mystery of Edwin Drood* (1985, with George Rose giving Dickens a Tony Award spin), *Anything Goes* (1987, the delightful Cole Porter revival at Lincoln Center starring Patti Lupone), and *Jerome Robbins' Broadway* and *Black and Blue* (both 1988).

The British musical invasion of Broadway that began with *Evita* (1979) and *Cats* (1982, based on T. S. Eliot's *Old Possum's Book of Practical Cats*) has continued with *Les Miserables, Me and My Girl* and *Starlight Express* (all 1986), reaching its pinnacle with the 1987 megahit *The Phantom of the Opera*.

In the straight-play category, British contributions have included *Equus* (1974), *The Elephant Man* (1978), *Amadeus* (1980), the Royal Shakespeare Company's *The Life and Adventures of Nicholas Nickleby* (which, for nine and a half hours, including a dinner break, transported audiences back to Victorian England and held them enthralled in 1981), and the RSC's 1984 productions of *Cyrano de Bergerac* and *Much Ado About Nothing.*

As for American authors, Lanford Wilson contributed such gems as *Talley's Folly* (1979), *The Fifth of July* (1980), and *Burn This* (1987); August Wilson stirred emotions with *Ma Rainey's Black Bottom* (1984), *Fences* (1986, a triumph for James Earl Jones), and *Joe Turner's Come and Gone* (1987); David Rabe proved he could be shocking and touching at the same time with prize-winning dramas like *Sticks and Stones* (1971) and *Streamers* (1976); Harvey Fierstein wrote the first out-of-the-closet play about gay life to reach Broadway, *Torch Song Trilogy* (1982); William M. Hoffman wrote Broadway's first play about AIDS,

▲ Ponderous pachyderms—stuffed, of course—roam the halls at the Natural History Museum.

▶ Many exhibits of dinosaurs are on display.

As Is (1984); John Guare gave Swoozie Kurtz and John Mahoney Tony Award-winning roles in *The House of Blue Leaves* (the 1985 revival of his 1966 comedy); David Mamet scored with two eccentric hits, *Glengarry Glen Ross* (1983) and *Speed-the-Plow* (1987, the play that brought Madonna to the Broadway stage); David Henry Hwang, a toiler in the Off-Broadway vineyards for years, finally hit the big time with *M. Butterfly* (1987), and Wendy Wasserstein did the same with her Pulitzer/Tony-winning *The Heidi Chronicles* (1988).

Year after year, Neil Simon goes his merry way, adored by the public and undervalued by the critics for such plays as his autobiographical trilogy: *Brighton Beach Memoirs* (1983), *Biloxi Blues* (1984) and *Broadway Bound* (1986).

More than ever, movie-making came back to The Big Apple in the '70s and '80s—an industry stimulated and aided by the Mayor's Office of Film, Theater and Broadcasting, established in the '70s. New York-shot films included *Rosemary's Baby* and *Midnight Cowboy* in the '60s; *The French Connection*, *The Godfather*, *Network*, *Annie Hall* and *Kramer vs. Kramer* in the '70s; and *Raging Bull*, *Arthur*, *Reds*, *Sophie's Choice*, *Tootsie* and *Moonstruck* during the '80s.

THE NOW AND FUTURE CITY

In less than four hundred years—from virgin forest in the early seventeenth century to a forest of skyscrapers in the late twentieth century—New York City has become, unofficially but unmistakably, the capital of the world. It is a multifaceted capital. It is the world's financial capital, the cultural capital of the world, the dance capital of the world, and the theater capital of the world (even English-born critic Clive Barnes agrees). Beyond

▲ New York City street fairs are always wall-to-wall people, and this Columbus Avenue fête is no exception.

(preceding pages) Columbus Avenue on New York's Upper West Side.

theater, New York is the entertainment capital of the world—with its concert halls, opera houses, dance centers, discos, jazz clubs, comedy clubs, and piano rooms—and it has recently developed into the cabaret capital of the world.

With more than 17,000 eating places, representing every known cuisine, The Big Apple is hands-down the restaurant capital of the world; and with its thousands of shops and stores in all five boroughs, advertising everything from antiques to zithers, it is most definitely the shopping capital of the world. Paris is still a power, of course, but when it comes to dressing the modern woman (and man), New York has the practical edge, the inside track, and so it has become the fashion capital of the world.

New York is an international transportation capital, a communications capital, a publications capital, and, if you consider the presence of the United Nations, a political capital. And to accommodate all the people who come to visit these "capitals"—the people who make New York the tourism capital of the world—it is, finally, the hotel capital of the world (with some 100,000 hotel rooms in more than one hundred hotels).

Culturally, New York is the treasure chest at the end of the rainbow. More than 150 museums are scattered throughout the five boroughs; and beyond the giants already mentioned (the Metropolitan, the Modern, the Guggenheim, the Whitney, and the American Museum of Natural History), there are scores of specialized museums such as the Asia Society Galleries, the Black Fashion Museum, the International Center of Photography, the Jewish Museum, the Museum of Broadcasting, the Museum of the American Indian, the New York City Fire Museum, the Police Academy Museum, the Schomburg Center for Research in Black Culture, the Studio Museum in Harlem, and the Jacques Marchais Center for Tibetan Art on Staten Island. There are two museums devoted to New York's history and culture (the New-York Historical Society and the Museum of the City of New York), and there are museums in each borough (the mighty Brooklyn Museum, the Queens Museum at the old World's Fair

▲ Brownstones are a disappearing breed, but they can still be spotted on the Upper West Side.

▼ The fanciful 1904 Ansonia Hotel, home to generations of music world greats, stands at Broadway and 73rd Street. Caruso, Chaliapin, and Stravinsky are some of the people who enjoyed the amenities of this elegant building.

▲ The "new" Metropolitan Opera House, which opened at Lincoln Center in 1966, displays two huge paintings by Marc Chagall in its foyer.

◄ This apartment house was called The Dakota when it went up in 1884 because it was the only building in the wilderness on Manhattan's Upper West Side and thought to be as remote as the Dakotas.

site, the Bronx Museum of the Arts, and on Staten Island, the Snug Harbor Cultural Center, Richmondtown Restoration, and Staten Island Institute of Arts and Sciences). New museums are constantly being added; the latest include the Museum of American Folk Art opposite Lincoln Center, the Children's Museum of Manhattan at 212 West 83rd Street, and the Lower East Side Tenement Museum at 92 Orchard Street.

In spite of the long history and celebrated reputations of opera houses like La Scala, Covent Garden, and the Paris Opera, the Metropolitan at Lincoln Center has become the mecca of the opera stars' world, and an engagement at Carnegie Hall is a guaranteed badge of success. Almost one hundred dance companies, large and small, either call New York their home base or play here regularly, including American Ballet Theater, New York City Ballet, Dance Theater of Harlem, the Joffrey Ballet, and Martha Graham, Merce Cunningham, Nikolais/Louis, Lucinda Childs, Erick Hawkins, Alvin Ailey, and Paul Taylor dance companies. In addition to these ticketed indoor performances, there is a cornucopia of free outdoor and indoor performances throughout the year. In spring, summer, and fall, such areas as Central Park, the Upper West Side, the avenues and plazas of midtown Manhattan, Greenwich Village, SoHo, and lower Manhattan (in and around the World Trade Center) teem with individual and group performers: mimes and magicians, tuba players and tap dancers, singers of all stripes, and string quartets. There is even a man who goes through the IRT's No. 1 subway line playing a pocket comb.

The world of New York entertainment is constantly shifting directions. A few years ago disco was king of the night, and

people flocked to clubs like Studio 54, Area, and the Red Parrot. Although far from dead, the scene is waning—at least as a fashionable pursuit—and cabaret is on the rise. Established performers like Elizabeth Welch, Julie Wilson, Margaret Whiting, Rosemary Clooney, Michael Feinstein, Paul Balfour, Forrest Perrin, and David Staller have made new careers for themselves in New York clubs like the Algonquin's Oak Room, Maxim's, J.W.'s at the Marriott Marquis, the Bemelman Bar at the Carlyle, and the new Rainbow and Stars atop the GE Building in Rockefeller Center.

Since personal style is always on parade in New York—on the avenues, in the parks, in the theater, in the clubs, even on the subways—it's not surprising that The Big Apple has evolved into the world's fashion capital. *Women's Wear Daily* is a bible to the style-conscious, and trendy publications like *Village Voice, Spy, Details* and *Paper*—as well as the strictly fashion magazines—keep careful notes on who's wearing what. Visitors to the garment/fashion district, along and off Fashion Avenue below Times Square, are often surprised to find it a gritty, decidedly unglamorous area, its streets clogged with delivery trucks, its sidewalks made hazardous by guys pushing handcarts loaded with ready-to-wear. This is the working area of the industry; for chic and charm, you have to go to the city's fine stores, shops, and boutiques.

Fifth Avenue is still the heart and soul of New York's shopping scene and the legendary names glitter as brightly as ever: Saks, Bergdorf Goodman, Gucci, Tiffany & Co., Cartier, and Lord & Taylor—with Henri Bendel, Hermès, and Laura Ashley just a precious stone's throw away, and Macy's still anchoring Herald

New York State Theater *(top)* at Lincoln Center is home to both the New York City Ballet and the New York City Opera. The Metropolitan Opera House is seen in the distance. Avery Fisher Hall *(bottom)*, home of the New York Philharmonic, the "Mostly Mozart" series and other events, was the first building completed at Lincoln Center.

▼ The interior of "the Met" as seen from the center Grand Tier. The dazzling crystal chandeliers, a gift from the Austrian government, are raised to the gilded ceiling just before the performance begins.

Square, along with the brand-new Abraham & Straus (where Gimbel's used to be). For boutiques and specialty shops, the leading areas uptown are the Upper East Side, especially along Madison Avenue and the Upper West Side along Columbus Avenue; downtown areas are Greenwich Village, SoHo (perhaps the city's hottest place for up-to-the-minute clothing styles), and, for the budget-minded, the pushcart, storefront, bargain-basement Lower East Side along such streets as Orchard and Delancey.

Because New Yorkers are a fickle lot, always searching for something new, this year's most desired restaurant may be next year's leftover. One season, nouvelle cuisine may be all the rage; the next, everyone is reading Southwestern, Northern Italian, and Eastern European menus. A carefully watched clutch of old favorites (mainly French) seems to survive from year to year—places like Le Cirque; The Coach House in Greenwich Village; The Four Seasons; Lutèce; The Oyster Bar in Grand Central Station; Le Perigord; The Quilted Giraffe; The Rainbow Room (now beautifully restored) atop the GE Building; The Russian Tea Room (where all the stars gather to graze); The Sign of the Dove; La Tulipe; and the "21" Club—but other, less self-assured, less well-run spots can vanish overnight.

If there have been definite restaurant trends in recent years, they have been: (1) an emphasis on fine food rather than glitzy decor, (2) a move to less formal restaurants—not too informal, just places where a trendy sports outfit will be as acceptable as a dinner jacket or evening dress; and (3) a move away from noisy places to quieter (not stuffy) ones—yes, conversation is back! There has also been a change in the location of the trendiest restaurants. Downtown is definitely in. The Odeon in TriBeCa (*Tri*angle *Be*low *Ca*nal Street) area started the trend, and it was soon followed by Chanterelle, Montrachet, Bouley, Rosemarie's, and the Duane Park Cafe. When that area got saturated, the NoCa (*No*rth of *Ca*nal) area began developing, with newcomers like Canal Bar and Alison on Dominick Street.

Greenwich Village remains a rich lode of dining experiences, with old reliables like The Black Sheep, Le Café de la Gare, Cent'Anni, Monte's, Chez Jacqueline, The Derby, La Gauloise, Ye Waverly Inn, Il Mulino, Ponte Vecchio, and El Faro. Newcomers that look dug in for the long pull include: Aggie's, Village Atelier, Union Square Cafe, Rakel, Rosolio, Telephone Bar & Grill, Melrose, Quatorze, and Everybody's.

Sad to say, there are only three truly dependable restaurants on the Upper West Side—Café Luxembourg, Café des Artistes, and The Ginger Man—and only several in SoHo: Raoul's, Elephant and Castle, and the flashy 150 Wooster Street, which looks like a graffiti-covered garage on the outside but is fun and funky on the inside.

In Brooklyn, three very special restaurants are worth crossing the river for: the River Café (for splendid cuisine and dazzling views of the Manhattan skyline), Gage and Tollner (for the freshest seafood in a landmark, nineteenth-century interior), and Peter Luger's (one of the city's best steakhouses). As for fine food at budget prices, one can't go too wrong at almost any of the dozens of places in Chinatown and Little Italy.

In the theater district, diners now have a choice of before- or after-theater dining, since several places now stay open late. Orso, B. Smith's, Jezebel, Rosa's Place, Le Madeleine, Tout va Bien, and Bellini are all night owls; and the long established Barbetta and René Pujol are among the early birds. The unofficial theater restaurant, Sardi's, in a class by itself, will be happy to see you early or late. In Rockefeller Center there are two notable newcomers: American Festival Café (plain) and The Sea Grill (fancy); and in Harlem the most popular spots are Sylvia's, Copeland's, and the Terrace Inn atop Columbia University's Butler Hall.

New York is so endowed with attractions, so crammed with special events that New Yorkers frequently play the tourist in their own hometown, especially when showing off slices of The Big Apple to visitors. In addition to the top sights already covered in preceding pages, no one should miss the architectural wonders of the city's diverse and distinct neighborhoods—wonders that can be seen only on a walking tour. Self-guided tours allow you to set your own pace, but the superb tours offered by such groups as the Museum of the City of New York, Landmark Tours, and Sidewalks of New York will let you see an area through an expert's eyes. Your choices range from "NoHo and the East Village" to "A Tour Named Jackie," which explores the exciting Upper East Side world of Jacqueline Kennedy Onassis.

If time is limited and you want to see as much as possible, nothing beats the efficiency of a guided bus tour; or take the Circle Line boat trip around the entire island of Manhattan, which shows you all five boroughs in three hours. Uniquely New York ways of seeing the city are the subway (underground), the Roosevelt Island tram (overhead), and the Staten Island ferry (over the bay). In the subway, try to stand at the window in the first car and watch the train go hurtling through the tunnels.

In your strolls around New York keep your eyes peeled for one of the city's greatest attractions: its wealth of celebrities. Legends like Jacqueline Onassis, Woody Allen, and Katharine Hepburn are frequently spotted, and you might even be lucky enough to catch the elusive Greta Garbo. Stage, screen, and TV stars are a dime a dozen in top stores and restaurants, and tycoons like Malcolm Forbes, Donald Trump, David Rockefeller, and Laurence Tisch often walk to and from appointments in

▼ Top to bottom:

Ballets of George Balanchine and Jerome Robbins are standard repertory at the City Ballet. Here is Robbins's *Fancy Free.*

The Nutcracker, one of the glories of the New York City Ballet, is performed every year at Christmastime.

New ballets—such as *Glass Pieces,* a Robbins work with music by Philip Glass—also find a home at New York State Theater.

The statue of Christopher Columbus at Columbus Circle *(left)*. The former Gulf & Western Building *(right)*, now Paramount's headquarters, stands on the north side of Columbus Circle.

midtown or the financial district. New York writers are all over the place—if you remember what they look like from their book jackets—and they include Norman Mailer, Arthur Miller, Tom Wolfe (always in a white suit), E. L. Doctorow, and Isaac Bashevis Singer. In any case . . . an invasion of privacy, such as a request for an autograph, is outré, although a slight smile, bow, or wave of recognition is perfectly acceptable as you pass by.

Certain annual events are mandatory whether you are a resident or a visitor. Among them are Chinese New Year (in late January or early February), the St. Patrick's Day Parade (March 17), the Easter flower display at Rockefeller Center and the Easter Parade on Fifth Avenue, the Ninth Avenue International Food Festival (mid-May), the Washington Square Outdoor Art Festival (weekends in spring and fall), the Feast of St. Anthony in SoHo (June), the JVC Jazz Festival (late June, early July), free Shakespeare in Central Park (July-August), the Harbor Festival and Fireworks (July 4), the Lincoln Center Out-of-Doors Festival (August), Harlem Week (August), the Feast of San Gennaro in Little Italy (September), the West Indian-American Day Carnival in Brooklyn (Labor Day), New York Is Book Country (mid-September), the Greenwich Village Halloween Parade (October 31), the New York City Marathon (early November), the Macy's Thanksgiving Day Parade, the Christmas Spectacular at Radio City Music Hall (November-January), the Big Apple Circus (November-January), the Giant Christmas Tree at Rockefeller Center (December-January) and the New Year's Eve celebrations all over town.

Incredible? Of course—and overwhelming, too, as in too much food on the plate. The secret is to take The Big Apple in small bites, always coming back for more. Otherwise the richness of

the city will defeat you. Above all, try to understand that the clash and clamor, the ranting and raving, the tension and troubles that you will often observe are part of what a throbbing, terribly alive city is all about. Renaissance Florence, for example, was constantly ravaged by strife and political turmoil, yet it produced some of the world's greatest art. Another example of what makes a city an exciting place to be can be found in James Forsyth's wise and witty play, *Héloïse*. The heroine, who is sequestered in a garden in Brittany, is talking to Théo, a messenger from her lover Abélard in the city. "Is there trouble in Paris?" Héloïse asks. Théo: "There will always be trouble in Paris . . . I hope."

As for your own attitude toward New York or the impressions you develop of city life, that is largely up to you. Remember that all great cities must be taken on their own terms, and it would be silly to expect London to turn into a city of extroverted back-slappers or Paris to start suffering fools gladly. Since the first metropolis was established, it has been a truth that there are city lovers and city haters, and neither group will ever see eye to eye. If trees and flowers and shady country lanes are vital to your well-being, New York is probably not the environment for you; The Big Apple is not scenic wonders, it is man-made marvels. But if you crave the stimulation of fascinating people, if you thrive on the mental gymnastics of good conversation, if even that homogenized hum of the city's myriad noises lulls you to sleep, then perhaps you'll find yourself taking root amid the asphalt and concrete, the limestone and steel. It would be helpful to remember the words of Plato: "Fields and trees teach me nothing, but the people in a city do."

▲ Ninth Avenue Food Festival, held in mid-May every year, clogs the thoroughfare and fills stomachs from 39th to 59th streets.
(following pages) The Brooklyn Bridge brings traffic to downtown Manhattan, to the door of the Municipal Building.

A.

B.

C.

D.

E.

F.

G.

H.

I.

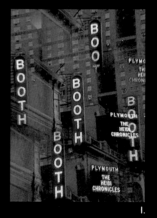

J.

K.

L.

M.

N.

O.

P.

Q.

R.

S.

T.

New Year's Eve in Times Square, the Crossroads of the World, waiting for the famous ball to drop at midnight.

INDEX OF PHOTOGRAPHY

All photographs courtesy of The Image Bank,
except where indicated*